p'h.

Goodmen:
The Character of Civil War Soldiers

For the goodman is not at home,
he is gone a long journey.
Proverbs 7:19

Goodmen: The Character of Civil War Soldiers

Michael Barton

The Pennsylvania State University Press
University Park and London

Portions of this book have appeared in different form in the following articles and are used with permission:

"Evidence on the Moral Socialization of American Children in 1864 and its Psycho-dynamics," *The American Journal of Psychoanalysis*, Vol. 37, No. 3 (1977), 235–239.

"Painful Duties: Art, Character, and Culture in Confederate Letters of Condolence," *Southern Quarterly*, 17 (Winter 1979), 123–134.

"The Civil War Letters of Captain Andrew Lewis and his Daughter," *Western Pennsylvania Historical Magazine*, 60 (1977), 371–373, 389–390.

"A Selected Bibliography of Civil War Soldiers' Diaries," *Bulletin of Bibliography and Magazine Notes*, 35 (1978).

Excerpts from William R. Taylor, *Cavalier and Yankee: The Old South and American National Character* (1961; rpt. Garden City: Anchor Books, 1963), are used by permission of the publisher, George Braziller, Inc.

Figure 1 in this book is adapted from Beatrice B. Whiting and John W. M. Whiting, *Children of Six Cultures: A Psycho-Cultural Analysis* (Cambridge: Harvard Univ. Press, 1975), p. xvi, and is used with permission of the publisher.

Figure 2 in this book is adapted from Martin L. Hoffman and Lois Wladis Hoffman, *Review of Child Development Research* (New York: Russell Sage Foundation, 1964), vol. I, p. 198, and is used with permission of the publisher.

Quotations from Wilbur J. Cash, *The Mind of the South* (New York: Alfred A. Knopf, 1960) are used with the permission of the publisher.

Library of Congress Cataloging in Publication Data

Barton, Michael.
    Goodmen, the character of Civil War soldiers.

    Includes bibliography and index.
    1. United States. Army—History—Civil War,
1861–1865. 2. Confederate States of America. Army—
History. 3. Soldiers—United States—Attitudes.
4. United States—History—Civil War, 1861–1865—
Miscellanea. 5. Character. I. Title. II. Title:
Character of Civil War soldiers.
E491.B37   973.7'4   81-139
ISBN 0-271-00284-0   AACR2

Contents

Acknowledgements

I am convinced that the first thing a writer should offer a reader of the *"new social history" is an apology. So I will repeat what the French historian Michel Foucault once wrote about his work:*

> *I know, almost as much as any other person, how "thankless" such research can be—in the strict sense of the term—how irritating it is to approach discourses not from the sweet, mute and intimate conscience which is expressed in them, but from an obscure ensemble of anonymous rules.... I know how unbearable it is to cut up, analyze, combine, recompose all these texts which have now returned to silence, without the transfigured face of the author being even discernible in it....*

But, of course, Foucault still believed in his work, as I believe in Goodmen, for the kind of truth it tries to tell.

Many people were my accessories. Michael Zuckerman, Murray Murphey, and John Caughey directed my doctoral dissertation in American Civilization at the University of Pennsylvania; Goodmen has grown, very slowly, out of that. Mike, it is insufficient to say, was a very kind genius then and thereafter. Klaus Krippendorf, of Penn's Annenberg School of Communications, taught me language analysis, but his sophistication and strictness do not show up here. James I. Robertson, Jr., Richard Harwell, and Charles E. Dornbusch advised me on Civil War diaries. At Penn State's Capitol Campus Melvin Wolf has been very helpful; he did most of the computer programming while I let him think I was learning it. He also came forward at the end to help me prepare this study for publication. Michael Bless, one of my former students, did much of the statistical analysis while he let me think I was teaching him. John Patterson, one of my colleagues in American Studies, stopped work daily on his own book so that we could argue about mine. Dozens of students helped me with the content analysis, and six of them should be cited for both their companionship and their calculation: Patricia Faust, Ed Ludwig, and Michelle Davis at Penn

State, and Julie Lerner, Jeff Claus, and Jon Wolfman at Penn. Doris Sklaroff typed the first draft, and Jan Russ typed the last, years later. John Pickering, my editor at Penn State Press, had the patience of Job in handling the manuscript, and also much of the Prophet's suffering. It was my luck that he was interested in psychology as well as the Civil War. Peter Ross Sieger, also of the Press, did his best to make my prose clear and pleasant.

The Capitol Campus Research Fund trusted me with a grant at an important point, and their Computer Center was generous all along. My campus also excused me for a year to complete the book.

Finally, I celebrate my dear children, Jonathan and Effie, and my remarkable wife, Jane Barton, M.D., not for any work they did, but for showing me, respectively, how character begins and how it lasts.

In spite of all this vital help, I wrote the book, and I know I must take the blame for any plain mistakes and bad ideas that stayed behind. But I am still looking for a way to assign responsibility for them too, and if I succeed in that ruse, I will be totally content.

Incidentally, I also apologize to the soldiers for any misunderstandings. I know you were live men, not numbers.

Introduction

Happy day, when, all appetites controlled, all passions sub-dued, all matters subjected, mind, *all conquering* mind, *shall live and move the monarch of the world. Glorious consummation! Hail fall of Fury! Reign of Reason, all hail!*
                                                        Abraham Lincoln

Andrew Lewis had the character of a Civil War soldier. He was a "goodman," a man concerned with conscience. He was born in Philadelphia, one of eleven children raised by Joseph and Hannah Lewis.[1] His father was a ropemaker, and Andrew became a plasterer, working in Columbia and then in Ebensburg, Pennsylvania. He was a willing soldier. He first fought in the Mexican War in 1846; his next enlistment was on June 25, 1861, soon after the Civil War began. He said he was forty-four when he signed on for three years at Camp Wright, near Pittsburgh, but he was really forty-eight. He was made first lieutenant in Company "A" of the Eleventh Regiment of the Pennsylvania Reserve Infantry, also called the Fortieth Regiment of Pennsylvania Volunteers. By November, 1861, he had a captaincy.

Andrew wrote often to his wife, Maria, and all her brood, and they, especially the daughter, Mary, were careful to keep in touch with him. To his daughter, plainly, father was a hero. "I cant find one more worthey," Mary wrote him. She was nearly seventeen, the eldest child, shepherd to her little brother and now main partner to her mother. She always pleaded for her father to return. Andrew admired his daughter so much that he apologized to her for the expensive plans he had made for her younger brother, Andrew Jackson ("Jackey") Lewis, who was nearly five. The father wanted the boy to be a West Point soldier. That would be a wise investment for them all, Andrew urged Mary, who seemed not to demur.

Surely Maria, the mother, was esteemed by them all, but her place now was to be practical. Andrew told her what to do with money and the crops ("You seame to think yourself quit[e] a farmer Well I am glad of that I tell you"), and which messages to send. He complained to her of sickness and the quality of his military life, that he needed more letters from home, and wanted more efficiency from the army. He told her all the gossip—the war was too profitable for some to be ended very soon, Jeff Davis was probably dead, and the army was willing to free Mexico from the French. They had been married twenty-four years, and had watched six children come into the world but only two survive. Andrew visited Maria in February, 1862, on a leave he requested from General Meade for reasons of her "ill health" and the need to handle some "fiduciary" affairs. Aside from this visit, Maria's letters, which have never been found, were the only contact he had with her that year.

Besides his family and his men, Andrew had to deal with himself. "Their is a g[r]eat many people may think what they p[l]ease of me," he wrote, "I hav as good a hart as the most of them has." But he made an admission to his daughter (and, coincidentally, to his wife, although he said it was something "your mother does not know") confessing that he had an "unconkerable passion" that "for an hour or too is worse on me than a whole yeare of hard work." Then, "often after it has subsided apearentaley to evry observer" he would be "sore from the effects of it." Perhaps it was a disease (he emphasized how "lazy" he felt), or his exaggeration of a bad temper (Mary mentioned that he had stopped swearing), or just his way of saying that he yearned to come home. In any case, he saw it as a vexing "passion" that it was his duty to overcome. Perhaps extrapolating from his own experience, he reminded Maria of her duty to the children, and he counseled Mary on her duty to practice writing. He wrote that he must do his soldier's duty, since he did not want his family to be ashamed of him. These were Andrew's perceptions of moral episodes in his own and in his family's life.

According to Samuel Bate's history of Pennsylvania's soldiers and General Samuel Jackson's diary, Andrew's regiment was a most active and unfortunate one.[2] It had the heaviest losses of any regiment in the Pennsylvania Reserves, as well as the eighth most serious rate of loss in the two thousand Union regiments. For the first year the men of Andrew's regiment mainly camped and marched, but then they fought at Gaines's Mill in the Seven Days Campaign, and then at Manassas, South Mountain, Antietam, Fredericksburg, Gettysburg, and the Wilderness. At Gaines's Mill they were surrounded by accident and had to surrender. They were exchanged from Libby Prison in about a month, but 46 of their men had been killed and 109 wounded at the Mill. Then about one half the group was killed or wounded at Fredericksburg. At the end of their enlistment in May, 1864, they hobbled home, 1179 men cut to 681.

Captain Lewis did not return with them. He was wounded in that battle at Gaines's Mill, near Richmond, Virginia, on June 27, 1862, just two days after writing his last letter (he had closed it by saying, "I believe that we are a going to hav a fight rit off so good by"). He was captured and had a leg amputated, but died shortly afterwards, on July 2. Mary remained single and lived in Lebanon, Pennsylvania, with her pensioned mother and, later, Jackey and his family, until she died in 1895. Jackey never went to West Point.

Dan Porter, who also had the character of a Civil War soldier, sent Andrew's wife a letter of condolence three weeks later (apparently he had sent her notice of her husband's death earlier).

> July 24, 1862
> Old Point Comfort, Va.

Mrs Lewis

In accordance with my promise I drop you a line. Surgeon DeBenneville returned yesterday. He reports your husband as having died from the wound received in Friday's fight. His leg was amputated, but not withstanding he died. I most sincerely sympathize with you in this your sad bereavement. The stroke is heavy, but we must bow in submission to the will of God. These are times that try men's souls. The sacredness of the family circle is broken, fond hearts are separated and every dear remembrance ignored. I can scarcely realize that he is dead, but alas I fear it is too true.

Allow me to write the inscription of him who now lies in the grave, in a southern clime, surrounded by traitors & demons to the best of governments. In memory of Capt. Andrew Lewis, who died from the effects of a wound received June 27th 1862 at the battle of Gaines Mill, fighting for the maintenance of law and order. No braver man ever lived—no braver man ever fell. No child of his need blush at the name of that patriotic, brave man. His character here was without a stain. In all intercourse he was most honest. He stood high in the regiment. Accept my heartfelt sympathy, and may God who pities the widow & orphan enable you to bear your load of grief & sorrow like the true christian who looks forward to a better & happier world.

> Yours very truly
> Dan G. Porter

The Victorian theory of character is exemplified in the words of those two soldiers. Its essence is the well-controlled personality: "passions" must be conquered, as Lewis, and Lincoln, said; there must be "submission," "law and order," "character," no need to "blush," as Porter said.

The essence of the need for controlling males in particular was

epitomized in the concept of the "gentleman." Such a man was no
mere dandy; he was, as his title indicated, a balanced, controlled
conjunction of both "gentle" and "manly" qualities. A revealing story
from a children's reader of the Civil War period bears this out. In
Lesson 33 of Charles Sanders's *School Reader, Second Book*, published
in 1861, a mother explains the concept to her son in exactly those
terms. The son had just hurt his little sister while playing with her, and
his mother rebuked him. When she told him to be more gentle, he
responded:

> "*Gentle!* how can boys be gentle!" said Joseph; "they should
> be hardy and rough like soldiers. It may be well for girls to be
> gentle; but who would like to be called a gentle boy?"
> "And yet, my son," said his mother, "in a few years, it would
> offend you very much if any one were to say you are not a
> gentle-man!"
> "O mother!" exclaimed Joseph; "I had never thought of
> putting those two words into one to make *gentleman*. To be
> gentle, always seemed to me like being weak and timid."
> "That is, by no means, the case, my son," said his mother;
> "for men of the greatest courage are often the most kind and
> gentle. But, perhaps, you would rather be called a manly boy
> than a gentle one."
> "Indeed, I would!" said Joseph.
> "Well, then," said his mother, "show yourself *manly* by
> being kind and gentle to all; be manly, not only by your
> bravery in times of danger, but by your courage in speaking the
> truth, even though in doing so, it may bring upon you blame
> and reproach."[3]

Another essay said the same thing more succinctly: "Remember that
to be a gentleman, a person must have a kind heart, and be of gentle
behavior, and polite manners."[4] Note that control of aggression has
priority even over courtesy in this formulation.

Books laden with such advice were as commonplace then as slick
self-help tracts are now, and they did the same job: solving doubt by
describing life and conduct cut and dried. Their theory is clear: Be
under control or be lost. My purpose in this book is to discover,
systematically, how that character theory was practiced by over 400
men during the Civil War, if only in the form of their verbal behavior
in diaries and letters. I smile at the description myself, but I would call
it a quantitative sociolinguistic case study in historical psychological
anthropology. This Introduction has described the popular theory of
good character as it was expressed in some exemplary sources. The first

chapter shows how historians have described the characters of Northerners and Southerners. The "hard" research begins in the second chapter, which compares the core values in Civil War soldiers' personal documents, and the third compares their character values. Chapter Four analyzes the writing styles of Northern and Southern soldiers, in pursuit of more evidence on their emotional styles. Chapter Five demonstrates how character was treated in especially revealing sources—Southern soldiers' letters of condolence. Finally, the sixth chapter gives a general explanation for the national character in the Middle Period and the different characters of Northerners and Southerners.

The book's main theme is the importance of emotional control in those times. It tests (and supports) Tocqueville's simple sentence, "The American of the South is more given to act upon impulse." It seeks group patterns by taking data from individuals. It studies national character by comparing regional characters. The differences between those regional characters are expressed in the terms of statistical analysis, though I realize that a "significant difference" for a statistician might not be a "significant difference" for a historian. *Goodmen* must oversimplify everything, but the response to that shortcoming should not be to say that the American character in the mid-nineteenth century is too complex to be summarized; rather, it must be admitted that everything we will ever know about our past will be, more or less, an oversimplified summary.

Finally, although the matter deserves more space than this, I want to say that after writing this book my respect for the old American character—mainly, to be self-denying—went up, while my respect for the new American character—mainly, to be self-realizing—went down. But if readers do not feel the same way after closing this book, that does not mean they missed my main points.

1 The History of Northern and Southern Characters

Clearly, societies differ in the degree to which they value self-control, or, to the contrary, open and intense expressions of emotions. These values have implications for the ways in which individuals judge their own feelings and behavior as well as those of others.

Erika Bourguignon

On April 15, 1861, the Milwaukee *Sentinel* published a rather unkind editorial. It said the South was lapsing back into "barbarism," that there "men resort to violence and bloodshed, rather than to calm discussion and courts of justice." It further accused all Southerners of being "impatient of restraint," so that they "indulge in a reckless and lawless disregard and contempt of all institutions of society or religion which obstruct the free exercise of their passions. . . . " What a contrast to the North, said the editor; his section was "mild, moral, peaceable, humane, Christian and enlightened. . . . "[1] Perhaps anticipating the *Sentinel's* truculence, the Chicago *Tribune* had presented a much more measured critique on February 21, 1861: its editorial said Southern men were only "semi-barbarous."[2]

Even Northerners who made a living by thinking instead of ranting believed that Southerners were primitive and madcap. Henry Adams, remembering the ones he knew at Harvard in the 1850's, remarked later in his autobiography that, "Strictly, the Southerner had no mind; he had temperament." Adams believed his own people were "sane and steady men, well-balanced," and that, "as a rule the New Englander's strength was his poise which almost amounted to a defect."[3] Another true Yankee, Ralph Waldo Emerson, said, in 1837, that the Southerner is "more civilized than the Seminoles . . . . a little more."[4] In 1844, in his essay "Character," Emerson said about the same thing, but more artfully and indirectly:

> Everything in nature is bipolar, or has a positive and negative
> pole. There is a male and a female, a spirit and a fact, a north
> and a south. Spirit is the positive, the event is the negative.
> Will is the north, action the south pole. Character may be
> ranked as having its natural place in the north.[5]

Even some Southerners agreed with their prosecutors. William
Gilmore Simms wrote to a northern friend in 1830, "But we Southrons,
you know, are creatures of impulse and prejudice." Perhaps that was a
mock confession, but another time he called his own people
"impetuous" and complained that "the true conflict of the Planter, is
with the flesh & the devil . . . . They yield. They submit."[6] William
Yancey, in 1855, simply called Northerners "cool" and Southerners
"ardent."[7] These observers of the South were applying the classical
theory of character—the standard was the control of emotion, and the
South was out of control.[8]

A review and summary of historians' accounts of these images of
character will provide a backdrop for the data on character which will
come later, and will also afford a better understanding of the country
that produced a Victorian theory of character and Victorian characters
themselves. Not a great many historians have tried to answer directly
the question of what the differences were between Northern and
Southern character. Most historians who have considered it have done
so coincidentally while seeking to answer the more general question:
How different was the Old South? It is hard to find a general consensus
in this area: Some say the South was quite different, and so was
Southern character; others say it was not too different, and neither was
its character. Some say the differences between North and South and
their characters were so large that they caused the Civil War, while
others say the differences, if they existed, had little to do with the causes
of the war. Many historians head for a middle position in this
argument. In any case, the question and its several answers have
occupied scholars for over a hundred years.[9]

There are two model answers to the general question, How different
was the Old South? The first one to be considered comes from Allan
Nevins and represents the traditional position in the argument. In his
famous work, *The Ordeal of the Union*, he concluded that the
differences between the Old South and the North were numerous and
substantial. Despite the country's strong tendency to "standardize its
moral and social values," he believed "two distinct cultures" had come
into existence by 1857.

White domination—what U. B. Phillips had called the "central
theme" of Southern history—was certainly a unique characteristic of
the old South, said Nevins. Its population was "one of the purest

British stocks" in the world. Its life was not just rural, but "rural after a special pattern," marked by plantations, great numbers of Negro slaves, and a preponderance of yeoman and poor white farmers. Its people were more often Protestant than Northerners, more prone to revivalism, and more reliably orthodox. Morals had a basic social purpose in the Old South, he said, while in the North moralizing was intellectualized. Each regional literature had its own tone, and, of course, there were differences in speech dialects. "Education for utility was steadily gaining ground in the North; education for character and grace held sway in the South." Government was localized and rather benign in the South; in the North it was more active and demanding. The South was an area in which "romantic and hedonistic impulses, born of the opulence of nature, had freer rein than in the North." More than the North, the South was a land where social classes were sharply stratified, and where the social structure itself suggested "vestigial feudalism." The Old South did not have a "body of intelligent, independent, thoughtful, and educated farmers," as the North did, and this fact, said Nevins, was one of the South's most unfortunate shortcomings. Southern gentlemen especially believed in, and exhibited, politeness, gallantry, and dignity, and thought their personal honor was even worth a duel if it were disputed. Thus, by 1857, the North and South were becoming "separate peoples." Political parties, religious denominations, and other basic institutions were breaking apart, and as each year thereafter went by, "the fundamental assumptions, tastes, and cultural aims of the two sections became more divergent."[10]

Other noted historians have given weight and elaboration to this traditional position. Eugene Genovese does so by stressing the importance of the slave plantation in Southern society. In the *Political Economy of Slavery* he contends that "slavery gave the South a social system and a civilization with a distinct class structure, political community, economy, ideology, and set of psychological patterns." Through the leadership of the planters, the South created an "anti-bourgeois," "paternalistic," "pre-modern" world view that was basically at odds with the "modern," "capitalist," Northern world view.[11] Today Genovese's Marxist answer is the most extreme one on this side of the question. The master of Southern historians, C. Vann Woodward, has written something similar in an important essay. He argues that the South's commitment to leisure, manners, and relative extravagance set it apart from the "bourgeois," "capitalist" North. He concludes that there was a "Southern ethic" which did not conform to Max Weber's description of the Northerner's Puritan "work ethic."[12]

The second model answer to the general question, the opposite, "revisionist," position, is best summarized by Thomas Govan. He recognizes that the South had such a "unity within itself" that it was willing to secede and fight a war for independence. He steadfastly denies, however, that there were "two civilizations" crowding each other in America by 1861. For one thing, Govan says, there was no Northern industrial capitalism absolutely opposing Southern agrarianism. Southern merchants, bankers, and planters were obviously all capitalists, and Northern and Western farmers were obviously not industrialists. The main economic dispute, he says, was between those Northerners who wanted internal markets for domestic trade and those Southerners who needed external markets for foreign trade. Variations in language, customs, and religion were minor, he argues, compared to those disuniting Europe, and wherever such variations obtained in America they were due to geographical and not political or social facts. He insists that the greatest cultural split was between urban and rural Americans, and he adds that this split existed in every section. The main sectional conflict, Govan concludes, was over labor systems: he would agree with Lincoln that everyone knew slavery was, somehow, the cause of the war, and not culture.[13]

Historians have likewise provided support for this second position. Edmund Morgan has argued that Southerners and Northerners shared the Puritan ethic as well as many other values until slavery forced them to disagree. He has also claimed that when the two sides criticized each other, they used the same values in their attacks.[14] Howard Zinn, in a provocative complaint, *The Southern Mystique*, agrees with its accusers that the South was racist, violent, pious, xenophobic, militaristic, chauvinist, and elitist, but he counters that "the United States as a civilization embodies all of these qualities." The South, he says, was simply the setting for their most intensive and dramatic evocation. "Far from being utterly different," the South "is really the *essence* of the nation . . . . it has simply taken the national genes and done the most with them . . . it is different because it is a distillation of those traits which are the worst (and a few which are the best) in the national character."[15]

There is a middle position in this debate. In some important essays collected in 1968, David Potter stated that "there has been much nonsense uttered about the distinctiveness of the South . . . But I believe that there are genuine and important features of distinctiveness." Much of this distinctiveness, he feels, was due to the South's "persistent folk culture." "In the folk culture of the South, it may be that the relation of people to one another imparted a distinctive texture as well as a distinctive tempo to their lives."[16] But in 1976, in *The Impending Crisis, 1848–1861*, Potter emphasized that all Americans were really quite alike: "Most Northerners and most Southerners were a farmer folk who cultivated their own land and cherished a fierce devotion to

the principles of personal independence and social equalitarianism
. . . . They also shared a somewhat intolerant, orthodox Protestantism,
a faith in rural virtues, and a commitment to the gospel of hard work,
acquisition and success."[17] But Potter knew his own uncertainty,
calling the South "baffling" at another point. Yet, we must ask, if most
Northerners and Southerners were "farmer folk," why did only the
South have a "folk culture"?

In an essay published in 1970, "The Two Cultures and the Civil
War," Carl Degler begins, like Potter, with the warning that "It is
possible, of course, to exaggerate the cultural differences between the
North and South before the Civil War." But finally, he says, "there
were differences between Northerners and Southerners that in truth
resulted in two cultures. . . . By the 1850's Southerners and Northerners
alike recognized that they were different, that two civilizations existed
within the United States." He believes the South was separate because
of the slave plantation and its consequences: "Slavery did more than
polarize political and moral opinion; it encouraged Southerners to
build a system of values and a society that were different from those of
the North."[18] But compare those remarks with what he wrote just
recently in *Place Over Time; The Continuity of Southern
Distinctiveness*:

> I certainly believe that the South was and is a distinctive
> region, but at the same time I think its system of values—then,
> as now—was quite congruent with that of the rest of the
> country. What set the South apart in the antebellum years was
> its commitment to slavery, but that commitment did not
> produce a world view significantly different from that of the
> contemporary North.

It seems he was aiming that remark about world view straight at
Genovese's work, but he creates a contradiction in the process: Were the
South's values "different from" or "congruent with" the North's
values? In this same book Degler says, "As early as the antebellum years
North and South had created a *myth* of differences that went beyond
the *facts* of difference."[19] Again, he fails to explain whether the "two
civilizations" which both sides "recognized" in the earlier essay were a
"myth" or a "fact." Potter and Degler could have been more precise
and systematic in their comparisons of North and South; cultural
anthropologists would almost surely insist that, by their standards, the
North and South were not "two cultures."

The specific question of differences between Southern and Northern
characters (or ideal characters or personalities) before the Civil War
must now be considered. No one is more interesting or inspiring to

read on the subject of Southern character than Wilbur J. Cash, author of the distinguished exposition, *The Mind of the South*. Its poetic enthusiasm, among other things, has earned it by now as much doubt as praise, but it still persuades.[20] To be sure, Cash begins, there may have been "many Souths," but "the fact remains that there is also one South." He says that "one" South was characterized by

> . . . a fairly definite mental pattern, associated with a fairly definite social pattern—a complex of established relationships and habits of thought, sentiments, prejudices, standards and values, and associations of ideas, which, if it is not common strictly to every group of white people in the South, is still common in one appreciable measure or another, and in some part or another, to all but relatively negligible ones.[21]

It was not quite a "nation within a nation," but "the next thing to it."

The dominant trait of this mental pattern was its celebration and practice of individualism—"perhaps the most intense individualism the world has seen since the Italian renaissance and its men of 'terrible fury.'"[22] One of individualism's corollaries was "an intense distrust of, and, indeed, downright aversion to, any actual exercise of authority beyond the barest minimum. . . ."[23] Another was the resort to vigilante violence: "What the direct willfulness of his individualism demanded, when confronted by a crime that aroused his anger, was immediate satisfaction for itself—catharsis for personal passion in the spectacle of a body dancing at the end of a rope or writhing in the fire. . . ."[24] And another corollary was the "tendency toward unreality, toward romanticism, and, in intimate relation with that, toward hedonism." Thus the Southerner, sings Cash, is "the child-man" in whom the "primitive stuff of humanity lies very close to the surface." He likes "naively to play, to expand his ego, his senses, his emotions." He likes "the extravagant, the flashing, and the brightly colored . . . he displays the whole catalogue of qualities we mean by romanticism and hedonism."[25]

Cash shows that Southerners expressed these emotional traits variously. See them in the poor white man:

> To stand on his head in a bar, to toss down a pint of raw whiskey at a gulp, to fiddle and dance all night, to bite off the nose or gouge out the eye of a favorite enemy, to fight harder and love harder than the next man, to be known eventually far and wide as a hell of a fellow—such would be his focus. To lie on his back for days and weeks, storing power as the air he breathed stores power under the sun of August, and then to

explode, as that air explodes in a thunderstorm, in a violent outburst of emotion—in such fashion would he make life not only tolerable but infinitely sweet.[26]

On the plantation these native emotional traits were expressed with more decorum in the concepts of honor and manners. Southern gentlemen

> served to bring into that pattern a certain discipline, to bend its native uncouthness, its frontier swagger, to seemliness and investment in established forms. Thus, for example, among these planters the tradition of fisticuffs, the gouging ring, and unregulated knife and gun play tended rapidly, from the hour of their emergence, to reincarnate itself in the starched and elaborate etiquette of the code duello . . . it was the only quite correct, the only really decent, relief for wounded honor—the only one which did not imply some subtle derogation, some dulling and retracting of the fine edge of pride, some indefinable but intolerable loss of caste and manly face.[27]

The gentleman took the native traits and tamed them into "rigid personal integrity"; they "saw themselves performing in splendor and moving in grandeur." Their concept of honor—"of something inviolable and precious to the ego, to be protected against stain at every cost, and imposing definite standards of conduct"—then trickled back down to the poor whites and yeoman in a simpler form "to propel them along their way of posturing and violence." The gentleman's sense of honor was also revealed in his view of his aristocratic obligations to those below him. This obligation he "professed with heartiness"; this he believed was confirmation of his "Christian virtues" and "selfless devotion," and "no group was ever more convinced that it was all so."[28]

These emotions in turn sought expression in social institutions. For example, Cash says that the Southern temperament sculpted its own religion. The man required "a faith as simple and emotional as himself . . . a faith, not of liturgy and prayer book, but of primitive frenzy and the blood sacrifice—often of fits and jerks and barks" (the trouble with the original Anglicanism was that it regarded "emotion as a kind of moral smallpox"). Thus the Southerner became evangelistic, in the style of a Baptist, Methodist, or Presbyterian. But the Southerner, especially the gentleman, was also a Puritan about his official morals, an aspect seemingly irreconcilable with the aforementioned traits. Cash says "he succeeded in uniting the two incompatible tendencies in his single person . . . His Puritanism was no mere mask put on from cold calculation, but as essential a part of him as his hedonism . . . One might say with much truth that it proceeded from a fundamental split in his psyche. . . ."[29]

Cash claims that in like ways the Southern traits were refined and expressed in the institution of politics—"a theater for the play of the purely personal, the purely romantic, and the purely hedonistic." Politics was

> an arena wherein one great champion confronted another or a dozen, and sought to outdo them in rhetoric and splendid gesturing. It swept back the loneliness of the land, it brought men together under torches, it filled them with the contagious power of the crowd, it unleashed emotion and set it leaping and dancing, it caught the very meanest man up out of his own tiny legend.[30]

Although they cannot match the power of Cash, there are other studies which match his emphases. Southern violence, according to John Hope Franklin's *The Militant South*, was due in part to the Southerner's "sense of personal insecurity." He was insecure because his political institutions were weak, forcing a man to depend on himself for his own protection. "Among men who already had a reputation for being hot-blooded and trigger-happy," this insecuritiy "doubtless had much to do with producing what was regarded as the peculiar temperament of the Southerner." But Franklin believes their militancy was most encouraged by their concept of honor—it was of "tremendous importance in regulating and determining the conduct of the individual." Honor "promoted extravagance," "sanctioned prompt demand for redress of grievance," and "countenanced great recklessness." It demanded protection of family and white women (this particular application of honor became more important "as the problem of sex and race became more complicated"). Coupled to his insecurity, then, was the Southerner's compensating grand sense of "personal sovereignty": "Ruler of his own destiny, defender of his own person and honor, keeper and breaker of the peace, he approached a personal imperiousness that few modern men have achieved." Franklin's work suggests that Southern individualism was, literally, rugged individualism.[31]

This same preoccupation with strong Southern emotions is present in Rollin Osterweis's *Romanticism and Nationalism in the Old South*.[32] He contends that the key was the Southern rendition of romanticism. Their romanticism, according to his "psychological analysis" of it, rested on heightened sensibility and imagination. Given that sort of predisposition, they worshipped feeling, glorified the individual, identified with nature, and exalted energy and power. The evidence for these traits he finds in their literature (especially their fascination with Sir Walter Scott); their copying of feudal customs such as chivalry, dueling, and jousting; their encouragement of heraldry, ancestry, and hospitality; and their veneration of women, militarism, and flamboyant oratory.[33]

Southern character has been such a magnet that there is a shortage of specific studies on Northern character, but there are a few noteworthy examples. Murray Murphey has systematically analyzed the psychological traits of Northern men in an exemplary exploratory essay, "by far the most sophisticated handling by an historian of the national character question to date," wrote David Stannard (though Stannard mainly had misgivings about the essay).[34] Murphey conducted his systematic interdisciplinary study with remarkable forethought, precision, and frankness. He integrated sampling techniques, historical child-rearing data, formal hypothesis testing, theories of personality development and aggression, evidence from autobiographies, methods of content analysis, and statistical reasoning. On the basis of twenty-three documents written by men raised in the middle Atlantic states in the early nineteenth century, he suggests that urban middle and upper-class males "worshipped God, home, and mother—not necessarily in that order—and were highly aggressive." He further suggests that the "extraordinary idealization of the mother" was probably due to the mother's use of mild discipline in the child's early years, while later "intermale aggression" was probably due to the father's use of corporal punishment and his generally stern management of his sons. Murphey agrees that these tentative conclusions sound "utterly banal," but he adds that they stand the possibility of being confirmed objectively. Unfortunately, there is no way of knowing if he would have found Southerners even more aggressive.

In a speech to the American Historical Association in late 1954, George Pierson remarked with insight but without concrete evidence on the nature of New England and New Englanders. Actually, he was talking about more than New England, because he maintained that his region and the North were roughly the same: "Between 1800 and 1860 a *Greater New England* was formed," he said. Thus, New England's values—"idealism, education, moralism, and humanitarianism"—became also the values of the new middle West. The historical character traits of Puritans and Yankees (and, by implication, Westerners) included "sense of duty," "passion for work," "extraordinary moral devotion," "resolution," "fortitude," "*will*," "choosy to a fault," "pessimists," "frugal," "introvert," and "suppressed emotions."[35]

The shortage of specific Northern studies is not so severe as it first appears because some histories of "national character" are in fact

mainly descriptions of Northern character. *The Lonely Crowd*, David
Riesman's by now classic interpretation of the American character, is a
good example.[36] Riesman argues that the predominant type of male in
the nineteenth century had an "inner-directed" personality. His goals
were mainly implanted by his watchful parents, and thus he had
intense identification with them and a strict conscience. He operated,
in Riesman's figure of speech, as if he had an internal "gyroscope"
which kept him stable in spite of disturbances around him. This
American maintained his direction because he felt guilty when he went
astray and could therefore "go it alone." He embodied the Protestant
Ethic: by occupation he was apt to be of the old middle class, "the
banker, the tradesman, the small entrepreneur, the technically oriented
engineer." (Riesman does not mention them in this context, but some
historians would consider successful farmers and frontiersmen also to
be types of "small entrepreneurs.") He was job-minded, mainly
concerned with things and their production. But he produced not only
things: "he must also spend his entire life in the internal production of
his own character." He was inhibited; work was more important than
sex. In politics he was a moralizer. Thus struggling for self-approval,
the inner-directed Northerner was protected against others, but "at the
price of leaving him vulnerable to himself."[37] Reisman does not say so
explicitly, but he implies that inner-direction was rooted in the North.
He does mention that in the rural deep South among poor whites and
Negroes one would find "remnants" of the older "tradition-directed"
character types.[38] He also notes that in the old South one might also
find feudal traditions, a stronger religion, extended family ties, less
optimism, and less social mobility.

Some studies compare Northerners and Southerners while pursuing
another purpose. In his *Modernization; The Transformation of
American Life, 1600–1865*, Richard Brown states that both Northerners
and Southerners had basically "modern" personalities—they all
wanted to be successful, and they were not archly conservative
"traditional" peasants. But Brown adds that the Northern personality
was a little more modern than the Southern. The ideal Northerner
"aspired to a masterful virility based on achievement, both rational and
moral," while the ideal Southerner wanted to be a "domestic patriarch,"
a "horseman," a "military officer," and a "man of courage and honor."
Acting like a Northerner (rational, calculating, and productive, all
crucial modern virtues) would have been "ungentlemanly" for a
Southerner, according to Brown.[39]

Edward Pessen's study of the opinions of foreign travelers on
Jacksonian America also contains a coincidental comparison.
Foreigners perceived the "Jacksonian character" to be natural,
generous, rude, grave, dull, cruel, selfish, insecure, thin-skinned,

boastful, practical, clever, laconic, unrefined, egalitarian, hypocritical, prudish, snobbish, traditionless, lawless, and most of all, materialistic. However, Pessen says, foreigners singled out New Englanders as being "cold" and Southerners as being "violent."[40]

There is one last place to look for comparative historical research on Northerners and Southerners, and that is in the literature describing the specific qualities of Union and Confederate soldiers. Bell Wiley has done the most prodigious research on the common soldiers of North and South; indeed, one of his articles concentrates on the very question of similarities and differences.[41] He begins by comparing the soldiers' national origins. About one-fourth to one-fifth of the Union soldiers were foreign-born, whereas only one-twentieth to one-twenty-fifth of the Confederates were born outside the United States. Wiley estimates that a typical Confederate company, composed of eighty to one hundred men, had from one to twenty illiterates, but a typical Union regiment, about the size of ten Confederate companies, would not have had more than a half dozen men unable to write and read. Northern soldiers came from a variety of occupations and included many skilled workers, while Southerners were nearly always farmers. The Union army had more men interested in political and intellectual affairs, although they were a rarity on both sides. Southerners were more emotionally religious in their diaries and letters. Immorality, says Wiley, was comparable in both armies, immorality meaning "profanity, gambling, drunkenness, fornication, and other 'sins.'" Wiley characterizes the Northern soldiers as being more "practical and prosaic" and more occupied by material and finanacial matters; Southern soldiers, he says, were more "fanciful" and "poetic" and humorous in their letters home, and so more likely to call their wives or sweethearts by endearing words. The majority of Northern men, says Wiley, fought to save the Union or destroy slavery, but the ordinary Southerner was at war to protect family, home, self-government, states' rights, and the Southern way of life, which included slavery. With those motives behind them, the Confederates were more enthusiastic:

> . . . after battle, in letters to the folk at home, they wrote more vividly and in greater detail of their combat experiences. In a fight they demonstrated more of dash, elan, individual aggressiveness, and a devil-may-care quality than Billy Yanks.[42]

But the Northerners had "greater seriousness" and more "group consciousness and team spirit." For them fighting required the "earnest and coordinated exertion of all those involved," for they believed there must be "as much efficiency and expedition as possible." These differences were expressed in two kinds of soldiers' battle cheers:

Southerners charged with the "Rebel yell" on their lips. This was a wild, high-pitched, piercing "holler," inspired by a combination of excitement, fright, anger, and elation. The standard Yankee cheer, on the other hand, was a regularly intoned huzza or hurrah. The contrast between Southern and Northern cheering was the subject of much comment by participants on both sides.[43]

Wiley argues that, in general, the common soldiers in both armies were "very much alike." Nevertheless, he has provided a most detailed and intriguing list of differences between two group personalities.[44]

An essay by David Donald on the Confederate soldier resembles Wiley's work very closely. In fact, Donald plainly admits his debt to him. He calls the Confederate soldier a man whose "story is that of all soldiers in all wars." He agrees with Wiley that the similarities between Northerners and Southerners outnumbered their differences; it would be "difficult," he says, to think of the Confederate as "unique." But Donald is forced to conclude that "the Southern fighting man [was] subtly and indefinably different. He looked the 'genuine rebel.'" He especially stresses the want of discipline among Southern troops, quoting Robert E. Lee twice: "The great want in our army is firm discipline," and "Many opportunities have been lost and hundreds of valuable lives have been uselessly sacrificed for want of a strict observance of discipline."[46] Part of the source of this lack of discipline was the Southern soldier's insistence on electing his own immediate officers. Consequently commanders might strive for popularity instead of authority. Donald also found in the Confederate army a great deal of resentment against both officers and enlisted gentlemen who might use their influence to gain privileges. Their army was "at the same time an extraordinarily democratic military organization and an extraordinarily aristocratic one." This was "the reflection of the basic ambivalence of Southern society itself."[47] Donald provides a very cogent summary of the common Southerner: "an admirable fighting man but a poor soldier," who was "the master of his officers" to a degree "almost unparalleled in any other major war." Quoting the Britisher, Colonel Fremantle, Donald says the Confederate had "a sort of devil-may-care, reckless, self-confident look." But this finally destroyed him, for he could not compete against the "highly disciplined northern armies."[48]

Pete Maslowski's neglected essay, based on his master's thesis, contains a systematic comparison of Northern and Southern soldiers,[49] although his main goal was to determine whether or not the morale of Civil War soldiers was similar to the morale of American soldiers in World War II (he found the two groups of men "amazingly similar" in this respect). His sources were the letters and diaries of fifty men, twenty-five from each side. All of them were "common soldiers," ranking from Private to Captain. In his content analysis of their personal documents he found that "ideological orientation" was low on both sides; in other words, his soldiers did not justify going to war very often by invoking values such as the "union" or the "preservation of slavery." Only 12% of the Northerners and 4% of the Southerners cited "love for country." Only 16% of the Northerners and 8% of the Southerners even made remarks indicating that they were "fighting for adventure." But Maslowski admits that there were some interesting, more substantial differences in their scores on other items. For example, Northerners more than Southerners had confidence in their own "stamina" (28% to 16%), had "confidence in our officers" (52% to 40%), thought they were in good "mental condition" (32% to 16%), "enjoyed army life" (88% to 60%), and believed that their own "officers were personally interested in us" (56% to 36%). At the end of his study Maslowski generally agrees with Wiley that the similarities of Union and Confederate soldiers outnumbered their differences.

This survey of about two dozen histories only shows the types of answers given to the general and specific questions. It is a representation of the best and most pointed scholarship. And since it has been estimated that there may be about 100,000 scholarly items published on the South, the North, and the Civil War, it would be wise and kind to cut the survey short here. But there is one more book to cover.

A country whose philosophers always counsel its citizens to examine their consciences and tighten up their self-control is a country bound to question its own moral qualities at large. The questioning will be even more intense and revealing than usual if the country believes it is morally cut in half. Before the Civil War Northerners and Southerners believed just that. They believed their characters did not match. William R. Taylor's *Cavalier and Yankee* describes those beliefs:

> The West was thought of as enterprising and independent, but, on the other hand, it was often portrayed as wild and unruly. The Yankee in his thrift, his industriousness and his asceticism was a praise-worthy figure in American popular culture; yet story after story dwelt as well on the mercenary, hypocritical and Philistine aspects of New England character. Similarly, the gay, pleasure-loving and generous-hearted Southerner won admiration for his indifference to pecuniary drives and his reputedly greater familiarity with polite culture and genteel ways; yet he, too, early became a cautionary figure in tales which revealed him as weak, vacillating and self-indulgent, or wild, vindictive and self-destructive.[50]

Men of South and North could act out these caricatures quite consciously. For example, Taylor writes that during the famous debates in 1830 between Senators Robert Hayne and Daniel Webster, "Each of these two men . . . became the personification of his region and adopted a suitable role. Hayne cast himself as a passionate Cavalier and slipped frequently into a military terminology of defense and attack. Webster was the transcendent Yankee, peaceable, cool, and deliberate."[51] To Webster, says Taylor, "'character' meant restraint, self-control, self-discipline."[52] What naturally bothered Northerners most about Southerners Taylor says can be "summed up by the word 'wildness.'"[53] Similarly, what Northerners admired most about George Washington, even though he was a Virginian, was the President's "self-control" and "temperate ardor."[54]

So far Taylor's commentary is not extraordinary. But the whole point of his book is that these images were part of a "historical rationalization," a "legendary past," and a "fictional sociology." "Few historians," he says, "would any longer contend for the idea of a divided culture as this idea was formerly advanced."[55] He seeks to discover the cause of these images, and he finds it in the anxiety both sides felt about modernity. They had "reservations about the direction progress was taking and about the kind of aggressive, mercenary, self-made man who was rapidly making his way in their society." Their solution, he says, was in searching for "a class of men immune to acquisitiveness, indifferent to social ambition and hostile to commercial life, cities and secular progress." The "legendary Southern planter, despite reservations of one kind or another, began to seem almost perfectly suited to fill the need."[56] Thus, Northerners, though proud of their achievements, were also vaguely ashamed of them and wanted to be Southern gentlemen; those same Southerners, while despising Northern capitalists, could not help but envy, indirectly, that region's historic values and modern prosperity. So, Taylor concludes, both sides were at war with themselves as much as with each other. The respective cultural stereotypes were the projections of those conflicting wishes and fears.

Thus *Cavalier and Yankee*, a landmark study, turns all the historians' arguments on their heads: to know the true character of Americans in the Middle Period, one must not take too seriously what they said about themselves and each other, but rather, like psychoanalysts, get beneath all that intellectualization and find the analysands' deeper motivations. As an aside, Taylor notes that determining the "historical authenticity" of those images of Northern and Southern character would be the subject of another investigation.[57] This is the purpose of the present research.

How do all these answers compare with one another? Is it possible to build internally consistent, comprehensive statements about Northern and Southern character and culture out of this farrago of studies? Underlining the general and setting aside particular comparisons, a majority opinion emerges which suggests that there was a common belief in a roughly Protestant character model and system of values, but a tendency for "typical" Northerners to have been more "Puritanical" and willfully controlled than "typical" Southerners, who seem to have been more "Romantic" and less controlled in their emotional lives. In other words, in Victorian America there may have been mainly one general theory of moral character but at least two distinct and patterned regional expressions of character.

2 The Values of Civil War Soldiers

The very vocabulary and grammar of a people reveal its psychic constitution.

Wilhelm Wundt

So far we have reviewed what a few contemporaries said ought to be the proper characters of both Northerners and Southerners, and what modern historians say were the probable characters of those men. Now we shall test the assertions of the witnesses and the historians. This chapter will seek to discover whether Northern and Southern soldiers expressed moral values differently—making this search through a content analysis of the core values expressed in the published Civil War diaries of one hundred soldiers.

There is a commentary in the Appendices on the method of content analysis and on the characteristics of our sample of soldiers. However, a brief description here of the methodology should make the data which follow more immediately comprehensible.

Content analysis is, in effect, a systematic method of sorting and counting written evidence. It makes explicit what many historians do implicitly. First, one selects the categories into which the content of the documents will be sorted. The categories for this phase of the study come from Robin Williams's modern theory of values.[1] Williams has written that core American values are (1) Achievement, Success, and Competition, (2) Activity and Work, (3) Moral Judgmental Orientation, (4) Humanitarian Mores, (5) Efficiency and Practicality, (6) Materialism and Passive Gratification, (7) Progress and Optimism, (8) Equality, (9) Freedom and Liberty, (10) External Conformity, (11) Science and Secular Reason, (12) Nationalism and Patriotism, (13) Democracy, (14) Individualism, and (15) Racism and Group Superiority. Williams's list was adapted slightly for this study: the category "Other Values" was added, "Religion" was added, and "Racism" was deleted. Six content analysts, or coders, studied Williams's definitions

Table 2 Distribution of Core Values among the Four Groups

Core Value	Percentage of Soldiers Expressing the Value at Least Once			
	Northern Officers (N=25)	Northern Enlisted (N=25)	Southern Officers (N=25)	Southern Enlisted (N=25)
Moralism	100	100	100	100
Progress	72	72	96	76
Religion	80	56	88	80
Achievement	68	52	88	68
Patriotism	76	44	68	80
Materialism	52	44	52	72
Humanitarianism	48	28	76	60
Activity	64	36	56	48
Efficiency	48	20	44	68
Other Values	36	12	48	56
Freedom	28	20	48	28
Equality	28	12	24	32
Individualism	28	4	40	24
Conformity	16	4	16	12
Science	12	4	16	8
Democracy	8	4	24	4

Democracy than Northerners. This appears to contradict the historical clichés about the natures of the two regions, clichés which held Northerners famous for all those characteristics. Before drawing any conclusions from this rather surprising finding, a further breakdown of these results is in order.

The core values were expressed by officers and enlisted men in the pattern revealed in columns 4 and 5, Table 1. The difference between the series of officer and enlisted scores, using the two-tailed sign test, is again statistically significant at the .002 level. The dominance of the officers is not surprising, since one might expect leaders to be more value-conscious than followers, by virtue of the officers' training and experience, their perceived obligation to uphold and teach values to their enlisted men, and their role requirements in general.

The final breakdown of the data, as seen in Table 2, shows how the four groups of soldiers—Northern officers, enlisted Northerners, Southern officers, and enlisted Southerners—differed in their frequency of value expression. The two-tailed sign test reveals the following probabilities for the relationships among the four groups:

	Southern officer	Southern enlisted	Northern officer
Southern enlisted	.302		
Northern officer	.266	.744	
Northern enlisted	.002	.002	.002

There are no statistically significant differences among the series of scores of Northern officers, Southern enlisted men, and Southern officers, but Northern enlisted men stand out as being significantly different from each of those three groups. The number of times enlisted Northerners use core values is so low that it is possible to conclude that they are significantly different from each of the other groups in respect to "system usage."

Comparison of the scores of the four groups of soldiers on each core value rather than on use of the whole system yields the following statistically significant results (significance in this case determined by a one-tailed sign test and a confidence level of .10):

(1) Southern officers used ten of the sixteen values—Progress, Religion, Achievement, Patriotism, Humanitarianism, Efficiency, Other Values*, Freedom, Individualism, and Democracy—significantly more often than Northern enlisted men.

(2) Enlisted Southerners used eight of the values—Religion, Patriotism, Materialism, Humanitarianism, Efficiency, Other Values*, Equality, and Individualism—significantly more often than Northern enlisted men.

(3) Northern officers used six of the values—Religion, Patriotism, Activity, Efficiency, Other Values*, and Individualism—significantly more often than Northern enlisted men.

(4) The remaining significant relationships are: Southern officers using Progress, Achievement, and Democracy more often than Southern enlisted men; Southern officers using Progress and Humanitarianism more often than Northern officers; and Southern enlisted men using Materialism more often than Northern officers.

*The most frequently mentioned Other Values were Peace, Home, Family, and Justice.

There are no significant differences among the four groups of soldiers on the frequency of use of Moralism, Conformity, and Science. Thus, in twenty-four of the thirty significant relationships Northern enlisted men are dominated by some other group. They are dominated by all other groups on five values—Religion, Patriotism, Efficiency, Other Values, and Individualism.

We have established the saliency of the variables of section and rank on the expression of core values. Southerners express them more often than Northerners, and officers more often than enlisted men. Moreover, when the effects of these two variables are combined, Southern officers and Northern enlisted men tend to be the most dissimilar groups; indeed, enlisted Northerners are unique. However, before discussing these findings at length, the possibility that two other variables—education and achievement motivation—might have had a significant influence on core value expression must be explored.

Education is a difficult variable to assess because there are twenty-nine cases of missing data. In Table 3 the distribution does not include the missing data. The sample is highly skewed in favor of highly educated men. "College" refers to all those diarists who were college students, graduates, or professional men when they joined their army; "noncollege" refers to those men who were known not to have a college or professional background when they joined their army. The value orders for the two groups are roughly similar—Moralism, Progress, Religion, Achievement, and Patriotism rank near the top in both groups, while the ideological values of Freedom, Equality, Individualism, and Democracy rank near the bottom. College soldiers dominate noncollege soldiers on those ideological values, especially in regard to Freedom. Noncollege soldiers, on the other hand, dominate Humanitarianism. Those particular differences might be worth some investigation, but when the two groups are compared in respect to their use of the whole system (again treating each pair of scores as a statistical trial), no significant difference between them emerges.

The missing educational data can be manipulated in two ways. The first involves re-coding all the missing data as being noncollege, on the assumption that the editor of the diary or the diarist would have mentioned such education if the author had attained it. When the data are manipulated in this way, college soldiers have a higher frequency of expression of twelve of sixteen values; a two-tailed sign test gives a confidence level of .118, which approaches the acceptable level of .10, but the findings are not statistically significant. Moreover, that result occurred only because of a most drastic manipulation of the missing data, which may have been an unreasonable re-coding.

The other manipulation requires splitting the twenty-nine cases of missing educational data proportionately and randomly between the college and noncollege groups; treating the distribution of the known sample as reliable, 61 percent of the missing cases are assigned to the college group and 39 percent to the noncollege group. This would be

Table 3   Core Values and Education

Core Value	Percentage of Soldiers Expressing the Value at Least Once	
	College (N=43)	Noncollege (N=28)
Moralism	100	100
Progress	77	79
Religion	81	79
Achievement	72	75
Patriotism	70	71
Materialism	60	57
Humanitarianism	51	68
Activity	53	54
Efficiency	42	50
Other Values	37	43
Freedom	44	14
Equality	28	21
Individualism	26	25
Conformity	16	7
Science	12	7
Democracy	12	4

(Missing Data: Twenty-nine cases)

considered a more reasonable re-coding than the previous one. The results of the second manipulation show the least differentiation between the two groups. The two-tailed sign test indicates that there is a nearly perfect probability that the scores could have achieved this distribution by chance alone. Thus education seems to have had no effect on the use of the value system in Civil War diaries. The bias in favor of high education in the sample of diarists is an interesting fact, but not a poisonous one for the research.

That education seems to have had no effect on valuation may be an artifact of the diaries' having been written during the war, when section and rank were bound to have more power over valuation temporarily. But it is also possible that a key insight may be drawn from this result: perhaps schooling only supported the evaluative habits which had already been established by one's social rank and section of the country, and perhaps that is all schooling was intended to do in the past.

Table 4   Core Values and Rank Progress

Core Value	Percentage of Soldiers Expressing the Value at Least Once		
	Always Enlisted (N=39)	Enlisted to Officer (N=23)	Always Officer (N=29)
Moralism	100	100	100
Progress	74	78	86
Religion	67	74	90
Achievement	59	78	72
Patriotism	67	70	69
Materialism	56	70	41
Humanitarianism	46	43	69
Activity	41	39	69
Efficiency	46	43	41
Other Values	33	48	38
Freedom	26	26	41
Equality	23	22	28
Individualism	15	35	28
Conformity	8	9	24
Science	3	9	14
Democracy	5	9	17

(Missing Data: Nine cases)

Examining value expression according to the soldiers' "Rank Progress" (that is, whether he was always enlisted, always an officer, or progressed from the enlisted to the officer ranks) gives the distribution displayed in Table 4. Rank Progress is employed here as a measure of achievement motivation in order to explore its relation to core value expression, the assumption being that those soldiers who made the most significant increases in rank may have been the highest achievers, and that they also may have expressed values most often. However, the two-tailed sign test indicates that the high achievers (Enlisted to Officer) do not differ significantly from the other two groups in frequency of core value expression:

Enlisted-to-officer versus Always enlisted	$p = .180$
Enlisted-to-officer versus Always officer	$p = .608$
Always enlisted versus Always officer	$p = .008$

In fact, those who were always enlisted differ significantly from those who were always officers, and this is an even stronger indicator of the impact of status differences on core value expression. Thus, the psychological characteristic of need for achievement has little influence on valuation in general, at least compared to section and rank. It is interesting to note, however, that on the specific values of Achievement, Materialism, and Individualism, soldiers advancing from the enlisted to officer ranks have the highest scores.

Returning to our main results, it is still necessary to explain the fact that Northern enlisted men (the modal type of American male) tended not to use the core value system so frequently as the other three groups. It could be that enlisted Northerners were using a different core value system than the one we measured them against, but that possibility is remote, since the enlisted Northerners' Other Values were not different from the remaining three groups' Other Values. Moreover, only three enlisted Northerners expressed statements which were coded as Other Values.

The possibility that the answer lies in the enlisted Northerners' different ordering of the core values is also unsatisfactory. Comparison of the four groups' rankings of the core values (based on the number of men in each group who used each value) shows that the four orders are quite similar. These results are in Table 5. Spearman's coefficient for rank-order correlation shows that the four rank-orders are almost in perfect agreement. Spearman scores on the six possible rank-order paired comparisons range from .86 to .96 (1.0 is a perfect correlation), and all six Spearman scores are significant at a confidence level of .01. Thus, it appears that enlisted Northerners simply used the core value system much less often than the other soldiers. Pursuit of an explanation for that "flattened valuation," may be aided by a look at the ways the soldiers kept their diaries. Table 6 shows various characteristics of the four groups' diaries. In this sample of published documents, Southerners kept diaries for a longer period of time than Northerners, and they also wrote the longest diaries. (Variations in page size or words per page were standardized for these computations.) Those figures could lead to the conclusion that all the results are merely a function of the quantity of written material which was coded rather than its quality. However, the last items in Table 6 undercut that conclusion. The former shows that, the sheer quantity of writing aside, the coders judged the Southerners to be verbose and the Northern enlisted men to be log-keepers. The last item shows that, when the soldiers are compared on the actual number of core values used per page, all the rates are remarkably similar except for the enlisted Northerners, who are simply not as expressive. These two results indicate that the four groups' scores on the use of the core value system

Table 5   Rank Order of Core Values among Four Groups

Core Value	Rank According to Frequency of Use			
	Northern Officers (N=25)	Northern Enlisted (N=25)	Southern Officers (N=25)	Southern Enlisted (N=25)
Moralism	1	1	1	1
Religion	2	3	3.5	2.5
Progress	4	2	2	4
Patriotism	3	5.5	6	2.5
Achievement	5	4	3.5	6.5
Materialism	7	5.5	8	5
Activity	6	7	7	9
Humanitarianism	8.5	8	5	8
Efficiency	8.5	9.5	10	6.5
Freedom	11	9.5	9	11
Equality	11	11	12.5	10
Individualism	11	13.5	11	12
Conformity	13	13.5	14.5	13
Science	14	13.5	14.5	14
Democracy	15	13.5	12.5	15

Table 6   Characteristics of Diaries

	Northern Officers (N=25)	Northern Enlisted (N=25)	Southern Officers (N=25)	Southern Enlisted (N=25)
Average Months Per Diary	7.9	9.4	12.8	11.6
Average Number of Pages Per Diary	31.8	25.5	42.7	36.0
Type of Literary Style				
Verbose	48%	32%	96%	64%
Plain	24%	20%	0%	20%
Log	28%	48%	4%	16%
Number of actual core values expressed per page	.68	.41	.69	.69

are a function of the qualities of the diarists, not simply the amount of material they wrote.

In summary, a content analysis of one hundred diaries of Civil War soldiers shows that the ideological values of Freedom, Equality, Individualism, and Democracy were less often expressed than the more prosaic values of Moralism, Progress, Religion, Achievement, and Patriotism. The analysis also shows that the soldiers did not use many other values outside this system, and that they expressed Robin Williams's core values in about the same order of frequency no matter what their section or rank. These results suggest that Southerners and Northerners shared the same core value system, a proposition which has been supported by a number of historians.

But some significant differences have also been uncovered among the soldiers. Southern officers expressed those core values most frequently, and enlisted Northerners expressed them much less frequently than any other group. These results were not due to how much the diarists wrote, nor to their level of education. Here is support for the proposition that Northerners and Southerners had different emotional styles in spite of their common value system.

3 The Character of Civil War Soldiers

> *[Northerners] are cool, sober, laborious, persevering, inde-*
> *pendent, jealous of their own liberties, chicaning, super-*
> *stitious, and hypocritical in their religion . . . . Southerners*
> *are fiery, voluptuary, indolent, unsteady, independent,*
> *zealous of their own liberties, but trampling on those of*
> *others, generous, candid, and without attachment or*
> *pretentions of any religion but that of the heart.*
>
> *Thomas Jefferson*

The first phase of our content analysis compared Northern and Southern soldiers on their core value expression, using categories from Robin Williams's modern work. This second phase of the analysis will compare the soldiers on their character value expression, using categories from a historical source—an antebellum dictionary.

Again, a brief note on methodology is in order. The 1851 edition of Noah Webster's *American Dictionary of the English Language* was, indirectly, a handbook on character.[1] Webster's categories for describing character may not have been the same as those operating in men's shabby taverns at that time (those categories may be impossible to recover anyway), but they were the principles behind much public discourse on the subject.[2] Checking and cross-checking the definitions of several interrelated words in Webster's dictionary—"character," "nature," "habit," "reputation," "moral," "bad," "good," and so on—yields the following system of categories for describing a good man. Such a man was (1) Moral, (2) Dutiful, (3) Skillful, (4) Kind, (5) Honorable, (6) Elegant, (7) Companionable, (8) Brave (9) Handsome, (10) Mild, and (11) Willful.

Seventeen coders each read a share of the one hundred diaries and isolated all the remarks dealing with someone's character. Each remark was then sorted into one or more of the eleven categories of character values, the explicit words about character in each remark becoming the terms exemplifying the categories. For example, the remark that

"Jones was a loyal man" would be sorted under Dutiful, and the word "loyal" would become one of the terms exemplifying the category Dutiful. Thus, we are able to state the contents of each category exactly (see Appendix III). A soldier was counted only as having used or not used a character value category, no matter how many terms in that category he had written down in his diary. This is the same counting procedure which was used in the core value analysis. Again, all the coders' results were pooled.

Finally, all the remarks about character were processed by a computer so that it was possible to manipulate them and retrieve information from them in several different ways. There is an example of this processing in Appendix II.

The first column of Table 7 shows the general order in which the character values were expressed by all the soldiers. The most commonly used character values, Honorable and Moral, relate to one's adherence to high social and ethical standards. Specific character terms used in these two categories include, under Honorable, "respectable," "fine," "splendid," "worthy," "noble," "just," "gentleman," "distinguished," and "esteemed," and under Moral, "decent," "virtuous," "good," "honest," "upright," "innocent," "righteous," and "wholesome." Each category also had negative terms—you were not moral if you were "wicked," "corrupt," "lewd," "profane," "drunk," "swearing," and so forth. Positive terms were more common than negative terms in both these categories. Honorable concentrates more on the exterior, on the way one is perceived by others, while Moral seems to emphasize the interior, the way one satisfies certain immutable standards. Honorable has its roots in medievalism and the aristocracy, while Moral has its roots in Protestantism and the bourgeoisie. So the character value system of the soldiers, at least in its terminology, was a mixture of two systems, one fading and the other emerging.

Those categories which were used moderately pertain to commitment (Dutiful and Will), control of aggression (Companionable, Kind, and Brave), and competence (Skillful). The two categories which were least used, Elegant and Handsome, would have been difficult to apply because of their nature—they are rare, largely physical, qualities. The category Mild was used rarely perhaps because it shaded into two other categories, Companionable and Kind.

The character values were expressed by Northerners and Southerners as displayed in columns 2 and 3 of Table 7. When the series of scores of these two groups are compared, the two-tailed sign test is significant at the .012 level—Southerners significantly exceed Northerners on the frequency of use of the whole character model, just as they did on use of the core value system.

Table 7 Over-all Distribution of Character Values

| Character Value | Percentage of Soldiers Expressing the Value at Least Once | | | | |
| | Section | | Rank | | |
	Total (N=100)	Northern (N=50)	Southern (N=50)	Officers (N=50)	Enlisted (N=50)
Honorable	76	74	78	80	72
Moral	73	66	80	78	68
Companionable	58	56	60	54	62
Kind	57	46	60	62	52
Dutiful	55	52	58	64	46
Will	53	40	66	68	38
Skillful	52	44	60	56	48
Brave	51	42	60	56	46
Mild	28	26	30	26	30
Elegant	21	18	24	26	16
Handsome	18	20	16	20	16

The character values were expressed by officers and enlisted men as displayed in columns 4 and 5 of Table 7. As with core values, officers exceed enlisted men on use of the character model; the two-tailed sign test is significant at the .066 level.

In Table 8, the data are broken down by four groups. The two-tailed sign test reveals that Southern officers significantly exceed each of the other three groups of soldiers in character value expression. They dominate enlisted Northerners at a confidence level of .04, Northern officers at a level of .002, and enlisted Southerners at a level of .012.

Comparison of the scores of the four groups of soldiers on each character value rather than on use of the whole system yields the following statistically significant results (significance in this case determined by applying a one-tailed sign test and a confidence level of .10):

(1) On four of eleven character values—Moral, Kind, Dutiful, and Brave—the only significant relationship was Southern officers dominating enlisted Northerners.

(2) On one character value, Skillfulness, Southern officers significantly dominated both enlisted Northerners and Northern officers.

Table 8   Distribution of Character Values Among the Four Groups

| Character Value | Percentage of Soldiers Expressing the Value at Least Once | | | |
	Northern Officers (N=25)	Northern Enlisted (N=25)	Southern Officers (N=25)	Southern Enlisted (N=25)
Honorable	76	72	84	72
Moral	72	60	84	76
Companionable	52	60	56	64
Kind	52	40	72	64
Dutiful	60	44	68	48
Will	56	24	80	52
Skillful	44	44	68	52
Brave	48	36	64	56
Mild	20	32	32	28
Elegant	20	16	32	16
Handsome	20	20	20	12

(3) On one character value, Will, Southern officers significantly dominated all three other groups, while enlisted Northerners were significantly dominated by all three other groups. This is the most impressive contrast between Southern officers and enlisted Northerners.

On the five remaining character values—Honorable, Companionable, Mild, Elegant, and Handsome—there were no significant differences among the four groups.

Again, the charge might be made that the results of the character value comparisons are only the consequence of the order of diary-lengths. But a comparison of the four groups of soldiers on their use of seven neutral words taken at random from the diaries, shown in Table 9, undercuts that charge. The numbers indicate how many diarists used the words at least once in a character evaluation. The four groups of soldiers are rather evenly divided on the use of the words "horse," "miles," and "marched." Where there are differences in the frequency of use—"afternoon," "night," "man," and "house"—they are not a function of the average lengths of the diaries. Thus, one can assert that when there are consistent differences in the use of character terms, those are differences caused by the diarists themselves.

Once again, consideration must be given to the possibility that enlisted Northerners used an alternative character model. This same

Table 9   Distribution of Seven Neutral Words

| Neutral Word | Percentage of Soldiers Expressing the Word at Least Once | | | |
	Northern Officers (N=25)	Northern Enlisted (N=25)	Southern Officers (N=25)	Southern Enlisted (N=25)
afternoon	12	20	8	4
horse	16	16	20	16
miles	32	24	28	28
night	32	40	48	32
man	40	56	56	68
marched	24	24	24	28
house	40	36	28	24

question occurred during the analysis of the earlier results on the use of core values, and the answer is the same: enlisted Northerners are using the same system, but there is "flattened valuation." This is apparent in Table 10, which shows the rank orders of the character values among the four groups of soldiers. Honorable and Moral have consistently high ranks across the four groups, while Mild, Elegant, and Handsome have consistently low ranks. Otherwise, there are some interesting differences: Northern and Southern officers have a tendency to rank

Table 10   Rank Order of Character Values among the Four Groups

| Character Value | Rank According to Frequency of Use | | | |
	Northern Officers	Northern Enlisted	Southern Officers	Southern Enlisted
Honorable	1	1	1.5	2
Moral	2	2.5	1.5	1
Kind	5.5	6	4	3.5
Companionable	5.5	2.5	8	3.5
Dutiful	3	4.5	5.5	8
Will	4	9	3	6.5
Skillful	8	4.5	5.5	6.5
Brave	7	7	7	5
Mild	10	8	9.5	9
Elegant	10	11	9.5	10
Handsome	10	10	11	11

Table 11   Distribution of Key Terms among the Diarists

| Key Character Term | Percentage of Soldiers Expressing the Term at Least Once | | | |
	Northern Officers (N=25)	Northern Enlisted (N=25)	Southern Officers (N=25)	Southern Enlisted (N=25)
kind	24	24	52	36
noble	12	12	48	32
gentleman	32	12	44	16
brave	12	20	44	40
gallant	20	8	32	8

Will higher than their enlisted men, while Northern and Southern enlisted men rank Companionable higher than their officers. These two differences are probably related to the groups' different roles in battle. However, the main point is that there is no significantly different ordering of the character values by the enlisted Northerners. Spearman coefficients on the six possible rank-order paired comparisons range from .64 to .89, and all the coefficients are significant at a confidence level of .03 or better.

Up to now there has been no examination of the frequency of use of particular character terms which were contained in the character evaluations in the diaries. However, a computerized analysis of the thousands of words used in all the evaluations reveals that there are five key character terms whose frequencies of use deserve close consideration. Those five terms are "kind," "noble," "gentleman," "brave," and "gallant." Table 11 indicates what percentage of soldiers used those terms at least once. These five character terms appear to be the critical signs in the "speech community" of persons known as Southern officers. Indeed, Webster's definitions of two of the terms whose frequency of use most clearly separates Southern officers from enlisted Northerners unlock much of the whole character model:

> **Noble:** Great; elevated; dignified; being above everything that can dishonor reputation; as a noble mind; a noble courage; noble deeds of valor. . . . free, generous, liberal, as a noble heart. . . . of an excellent disposition. . . .

> **Gallant:** Gay; well-dressed; showy; splendid; magnificent. . . . Brave; high-spirited; courageous; heroic; magnanimous; as a gallant youth; a gallant officer. . . . fine; noble. . . . courtly, civil, polite and attentive to ladies; courteous.

Clearly, "gallant" and "noble" blend with one another, and at the same time summon other values in the whole character model, such as Honorable, Brave, Kind, Will, Mild, and Elegant. Webster's definitions of those two terms also remind one of the historians' descriptions of the archetypal Southerner. This whole study does not rest on the use of these two terms, but they represent a distillation of much of the analysis of the language of character evaluation.

Table 12 presents the results of a chi-square test on the use of these five key terms in the diaries. According to the test, the dominance of Southern officers over enlisted Northerners is significant on the use of every term. Among the other groups, however, the levels of statistical differences are usually not significant, even though the direction of the counts always favors the dominance of Southern officers. The term "noble" differentiates the groups of diarists most often and most effectively.

When the core and character value analyses are compared, the patterns of results support one another. In the case of core value expression, enlisted Northerners were dominated by every other group, especially Southern officers; on character value expression, Southern officers dominated enlisted Northerners when there were significant differences among the groups. Northern officers and enlisted Southerners are in the middle of that contrast, not varying too often from one another. The character model, like the core value system, seems to have been a shared national standard, though Southern officers stressed its Cavalier features. The various levels of participation in the core value system and the character model support the hypothesis that enlisted Northerners and Southern officers had distinct emotional configurations. Recall especially the results on the character value of Will. Southern officers used it the most, enlisted Northerners least. This could be a useful index of the "amount" of emotion that was invested in a diary by its author.

How do these two value analyses mesh with historians' opinions of the Old South and North? It appears that Southern officers were the most enthusiastic Americans in their value expressions and that enlisted Northerners, though they were the largest group in the country at that time, were the least enthusiastic. Thus, both sides in the "two civilizations" debate have a point to make—the Southern gentlemen were the model Americans, but they were, indeed, different from the modal Americans, the enlisted Northerners.

In order to further test how the results on the five key character terms hold up, evidence from 200 collections of Civil War letters (over 3200 letters in all) was included, doubling the size of the sample and putting 50 soldiers instead of 25 into each of the four groups, because good letters are more readily available than good diaries. The sample of

Table 12 Statistics on Key Terms in Diaries

Chi-Squares (χ^2) and Levels of Significance (p)

Groups Being Compared	kind χ^2	p	noble χ^2	p	gentle-man χ^2	p	brave χ^2	p	gallant χ^2	p
Southern Officers vs. Northern Enlisted	6.14	.02	7.71	.01	6.35	.02	3.31	.10	4.50	.05
Southern Officers vs. Northern Officers	6.14	.02	7.71	.01	.76	NS	6.35	.02	.94	NS
Southern Officers vs. Southern Enlisted	1.30	NS	1.33	NS	4.67	.05	.00	NS	4.50	.05
Northern Enlisted vs. Northern Officers	.00	NS	.00	NS	2.91	.10	.60	NS	1.50	NS
Northern Enlisted vs. Southern Enlisted	.86	NS	2.91	.10	.00	NS	2.38	.20	.00	NS
Northern Officers vs. Southern Enlisted	.86	NS	2.91	.10	1.75	.20	5.09	.05	1.50	NS
North vs. South	4.46	.05	10.19	.01	.83	NS	8.21	.01	.64	NS
Officers vs. Enlisted	.71	NS	.83	NS	7.48	.01	.00	NS	5.74	.02

(NS = not significant)

Table 13   Distribution of Key Terms among the Letter-writers

Key Character Term	Percentage of Soldiers Expressing the Term at Least Once			
	Northern Officers (N=50)	Northern Enlisted (N=50)	Southern Officers (N=50)	Southern Enlisted (N=50)
kind	38	24	52	36
noble	34	14	34	20
gentleman	40	24	46	12
brave	50	24	52	28
gallant	32	4	38	18

letters is also useful because it is a more accurate representation of the national population of males, letter-writers in the sample tending not to be so highly educated as the diarists.

Table 13 shows how the four groups of letter-writers used the five key terms. Again, the Southern officers used them most often, the enlisted Northerners least often. While "noble" was the best discriminator among the diarists, the key term "gallant" is the best discriminator in the letters. Notice its extraordinarily low use by enlisted Northerners— only 2 out of 50. These relationships are brought out more precisely in Table 14, which applies the chi-square test to the key word counts in the letters. As in the diaries, the dominance of Southern officers over enlisted Northerners is statistically significant on every key term in the letters. But these calculations also present a new finding: the strongest difference among letter-writers in the use of the five terms occurs between officers and enlisted men; the officers seem much more likely to have used character terms in their letters than in their diaries. Perhaps this fact is explained by the different functions those documents may have had for the officers—apparently, they were more likely to report on the conduct of their men when they wrote home than when they wrote "to themselves." Yet, the crucial comparison still stands: Southern officers were likely to evaluate character anytime they wrote anything, while ordinary Northerners rarely touched on it, especially if it might be called "noble" or "gallant" conduct. The 75 enlisted Northerners used those two terms an absolute total of only 17 times in their diaries and letters, while the 75 Southern officers used the two terms 132 times. The Northern officers used them 72 times, the enlisted Southerners 46 times. To be more concrete, Ulysses S. Grant used not one of the key character terms in 23 letters to his wife and family, but Robert E. Lee used them 10 times in 31 letters to his wife, including the crucial Southern word "gallant."

Table 14 Statistics on Key Terms in Letters

Chi-Squares (x^2) and Levels of Significance (p)

Groups Being Compared	kind x^2	kind p	noble x^2	noble p	gentle-man x^2	gentle-man p	brave x^2	brave p	gallant x^2	gallant p
Southern Officers vs. Northern Enlisted	8.32	.01	5.48	.02	5.32	.05	8.32	.01	17.42	.001
Southern Officers vs. Northern Officers	1.98	.20	.00	NS	.37	NS	.00	NS	.40	NS
Southern Officers vs. Southern Enlisted	2.60	.20	2.49	.20	14.04	.001	6.00	.02	4.96	.05
Northern Enlisted vs. Northern Officers	2.29	.20	5.48	.02	2.94	.10	7.25	.01	13.28	.001
Northern Enlisted vs. Southern Enlisted	1.71	.20	.64	NS	2.43	.20	.00	NS	5.01	.05
Northern Officers vs. Southern Enlisted	.04	NS	2.49	.20	10.19	.01	5.09	.05	2.61	.20
North vs. South	3.61	.10	.24	NS	.00	NS	.00	NS	2.82	.10
Officers vs. Enlisted	4.80	.05	7.61	.01	14.74	.001	13.20	.001	16.26	.001

(NS = not significant)

4 The Style of Character

The Athenian citizen is reputed among all the Hellenes to be a great talker, whereas Sparta is renowned for brevity, and the Cretans have more wit than words. Now I am afraid of appearing to elicit a very long discourse out of a very small matter.

Plato

The comparative analysis of core and character value expression in Civil War diaries and letters has told as much about the soldiers' emotions as it has about their morals. It is therefore necessary to study the soldiers' styles of written expression even more closely. This chapter will investigate whether differences between the more expressive Southerners and the less expressive Northerners still hold when linguistic analysis is performed on an unconscious form of behavior—not what they wrote, but how they wrote.

Plato may have been the first to recognize that different groups of people can have different styles of communicating. His general insight—that the processes of speaking and writing, in themselves, will reveal culture and personality—has lately been used by psychologists who wish to study the expression of emotion in the language of their patients. For example, Lorenz and Cobb have written that "hysterics" use more pronouns (especially "I"), verbs, adjectives, and adverbs than "normals," but that "obsessive-compulsive" persons use fewer adjectives, fewer conjunctions, and fewer articles of speech than "normals."[1] Irwin Berg examined how the stylistic traits of one patient's speech changed as his mental condition improved: his references to himself ("ego" pronouns) decreased, his reference to others ("empathic" pronouns) increased, and his use of "expletive" words (words beginning with harsh-sounding letters such as "b," "k," and "f") decreased. To Berg these changes in speech habits meant that the patient was becoming less self-centered, more aware of others, and less aggressive.[2] Other studies have shown that schizophrenic patients invent new words ("neologisms"), but that "normals" use a greater variety of words in both their speaking and writing.[3] These measures are useful because they precisely record those subtle behavioral and linguistic changes which are beyond the control of the patient.

Some of these methods have been borrowed for this study, not to look for insanity among Southerners and Northerners, but to see if "normal" populations might also vary from one another along these lines, and if their variations in styles of communicating might have psychological implications (even if not exactly the same as those suggested by clinical studies). If some "verbose" men seemed more willing than "laconic" men to express core and character values in their personal documents, then perhaps those same men were more willing than others to express themselves in the act of writing, as measured by their traits of style. This exercise can be another way, then, of developing our knowledge of the ways Victorians controlled their impulses.

To that end, coders counted the following stylistic traits in 292 published Civil War diaries and letter collections:

(1) The rate at which entries were made in the diary, expressed as "days between entries." A rate of 1.0 would mean that the diarist made an entry each day, while a rate higher than that would mean the diarist was less regular in making entries. This measure is used to judge how habitual and methodical the diarist might be in his approach to life and how much he planned and scrutinized his behavior. In one sense, all diarists might be considered methodical, but clearly some are more methodical than others. Some diaries, of course, might have provoked regular entries because they were printed with a space for writing for each day of the year, as modern diaries are printed. But there is no reason to believe that any one group of soldiers was more likely to have used these types of printed diaries than any other group. Most actual diaries, according to the editors of published Civil War diaries, were books without printed dates, and even if they did have printed dates in them, the soldier would still have to have decided to fill in all the dates in order to receive a rating of 1.0. The possibility also exists that some soldiers may have been methodical diarists simply because they were in camp most of the time with nothing else to do but write, while other soldiers might appear to be less methodical simply because they were too busy fighting and marching to keep daily entries. But again, there is no reason to believe that any one group of soldiers had those advantages or disadvantages more than another group. Any differences in the rates will therefore be treated as possible indicators of the dominance of "methodical" personalities or "non-methodical" personalities among the various groups of soldiers.

(2) The average number of words per diary entry and the average number of words per letter. These two statistics are intended to measure the sheer amount of verbal expression by diarists and letter-writers. The results, of course, could be influenced by the size and amount of paper available for a letter, the space available in a diary, and the simple amount of time available for writing, all factors having nothing to do with personality (though one could argue that a soldier who has the "need" to write will always find time and space to do it). The results could also be influenced by the amount of editing done by the editor of published diaries and letters (though coders were careful to count words only where the text had not been edited). But again, there is no reason to believe that any one group of soldiers had these "problems" more than any other group.

(3) The average number of syllables per 100 words in the diaries and letters. This can be taken as a measure of the relative concreteness of the soldiers' writing—the fewer syllables, the more concreteness.

(4) The average number of words per sentence. The same principles apply here as in the previous statistic—verbose or romantic soldiers might use significantly more words in a sentence than laconic, concrete, practical soldiers. (Some of the sentences in the less articulate documents were strung together without punctuation, so the coders inserted punctuation where thoughts were completed, following precedent in those documents and reasonable rules on sentence construction.)

(5) The percentage of incomplete sentences per 100 words. This can be employed as another measure of the degree of emotional expressiveness in writing: incomplete sentences would be more likely uttered by laconic writers, while complete sentences would be more characteristic of expressive writers. Note that the concern here is not with "bad grammar," but with sentences or phrases wherein the subject or predicate has consciously been left out, as in "Marched five miles," or "Colonel Jones a kind man." Educated as well as uneducated men might write this way if they were psychologically disposed to express themselves this way.

(6) The percentage of negative words ("no," "not," "never," "nothing," "none," and all "n't" contractions) per 100 words. Berg suggests that there will be more negative words from a person in "emotional turmoil" who "finds difficulty in saying specifically what his problem consists of."[4]

(7) The percentage of explosive initial sounds per 100 words ("b," "k," "c," "f," "p," and "s"). These hard or hissing sounds are said to be

expressions of aggressiveness, usually disguised and unconscious but sometimes open and conscious. Sanford says that "a predilection for the explosive 'p' sound may indicate that the speaker is symbolically indulging in some manner of noxious emission upon his audience"[5] (remember comedy routines from vaudeville in which one nasty fellow literally spits "p's" at his unfortunate partner). Also, most brief curses or obscene expletives begin with these harsh sounds ("d" for "damn," "darn," "drat," and so forth is missing here, but let us be content to follow Berg's scheme).

(8) The percentage of ego pronouns per 100 words. The dominance of ego pronouns ("I," "me," "myself," "mine") over other types of pronouns could indicate a high degree of self-consciousness, ranging from self-pity to great self-confidence. This will be a rough indicator of "individualism."

(9) The percentage of solidarity pronouns per 100 words. The dominance of solidarity pronouns ("we," "us," "our," "ours," "ourselves") over other types of pronouns in a document, especially ego pronouns, could suggest that group identity was more important to the writer than individual identity. Indeed, the comparison of rates of ego and solidarity pronouns may likely be a telling one, since a writer is usually free to use one type of pronoun or the other without changing the content of his statement ("I ate" or "we ate"; "I marched" or "we marched"). He thus reveals his disposition toward self and others. As one pronoun rate goes up, the other rate ought to go down in a group of documents. The dominance of solidarity pronouns can be taken as a rough indicator of a group's commitment to "conformity."

(10) The percentage of detached pronouns per 100 words. These pronouns ("he," "she," "him," "her," "his," "hers," "himself," "herself," "you," "your," "yours," "yourself," "yourselves," "they," "them," "their," "theirs," "themselves") are, in a sense, the "leftover" pronouns. The dominance of detached pronouns could indicate the degree of concern for others alone rather than one's self or the group which includes one's self as a member. Berg suggests that in psychotherapy a "client's" transition from the exclusive use of ego pronouns to the use of some detached pronouns indicates the ability to take the point of view of others (Berg lumps detached pronouns together with solidarity pronouns and calls then all "empathic" pronouns, but that tactic is not so useful here).

The methods for this phase of the study can be described quickly. Random samples of text were first taken from 185 Civil War diaries— 53 Northern officers, 35 Southern officers, 62 enlisted Northerners, and

Table 15   Bases for Style Counts in Diaries

Variable	Group Averages			
	Northern Officers (N=53)	Northern Enlisted (N=62)	Southern Officers (N=35)	Southern Enlisted (N=35)
Average Number of Entries Counted per Diary	17.4	19.3	17.6	18.7
Ranges in Number of Entries Chosen per Diary	3-30	6-43	3-20	4-20
Average Number of Words Counted per Diary	1896.5	1268.0	1598.1	1799.1
Ranges in Number of Words Counted per Diary	164-11,021	234-4816	165-5455	287-6544

35 enlisted Southerners. Diary entries were chosen at random from those samples and all the words in those entries were counted for style. The modal number of entries chosen was 20, but if the entries were very long or very brief, that number could vary up or down accordingly. The coders were told not to take strings of words from just one entry or from entries immediately following one another; the point was to treat each entry as a separate unit of prose or expression. Then style counts from several variously sized random entries were combined to give an average set of counts for each diary. Then those average counts were combined to given an average count on the trait for each group of soldiers. The coders were told to count a total of at least 100 words from each of at least three entries. Those minimums, however, only needed to be applied to those diaries with the fewest words or the fewest entries, a small number of cases in all. The average number of words counted for style per diary was 1640, and the average number of entries chosen for counting was 18.3 per diary. The breakdown on these variables for the four groups of diarists is shown in Table 15.

In sum, about 300,000 words were included in the style counts of the 185 diaries. Uniform counting procedures were established for the coders (dates of entries were not counted, numbers, abbreviations, and hyphenated words were each counted as one word, and so forth).

Random samples of text were then taken from 107 letter collections. The texts of the letters were also sampled as if each letter were a distinct unit of prose, but the procedures were simpler, and smaller numbers of words were used. A mean and modal number of five letters were chosen at random from each soldier for counting; the range of letters chosen per soldier was 1 to 10. If there were five or more letters chosen, then the first 100 words in each of those letters were the basis for the style count; if less than five letters could be chosen, then the first 100 words in each of the available letters were chosen and additional strings of 100 words were randomly chosen from within the available letters, making a total of five strings (coders were allowed to extend their counts beyond 100 words if they needed to complete counting on a sentence). All the style counts are therefore based on at least five strings of 100 or more words from each letter collection. A total of 60,000 words was counted from the 107 letter collections (about 1800 letters in all). There were 32 Northern officers, 23 Southern officers, 28 enlisted Northerners, and 24 enlisted Southerners in the sample of letter-writers. The complete letters averaged 546 words in length: Northern officers, 542.3 words; Southern officers, 577.9 words; enlisted Northerners, 637.2 words; enlisted Southerners, 426.4 words (these counts were taken only if the soldier wrote five or more letters).

The results of the diary counts are shown in Table 16. A statistical test, two-way analysis of variance, shows the following differences among diarists and their levels of statistical significance:

(1) Northerners tended to write entries in their diaries more methodically than Southerners ($p=.05$), with the greatest difference between Northern officers (one entry every 1.76 days) and Southern officers (one entry every 3.27 days).

(2) Officers tended to write more words per diary entry than enlisted men ($p=.01$), with the greatest difference between Northern officers (139.4 words) and enlisted Northerners (69.6 words).

(3) There were no significant differences in syllables per 100 words.

(4) Southerners tended to use more words per sentence than Northerners ($p=.10$), with the greatest difference between Southern officers (14.9 words) and enlisted Northerners (12.4 words).

(5) Northerners tended to write more incomplete sentences than Southerners ($p=.05$), with the greatest difference between enlisted Northerners (42.8%) and Southern officers (28.3%).

(6) There were no significant differences among the diarists on the use of negative words.

(7) Northerners tended to use more explosive initial sounds than Southerners ($p=.05$), with the greatest difference between Northern officers (19.4%) and Southern officers (16.3%).

Table 16   Characteristics of Diary Style

Variable	Group Averages			
	Northern Officers (N=53)	Northern Enlisted (N=62)	Southern Officers (N=35)	Southern Enlisted (N=35)
Days Between Entries	1.76	2.42	3.27	2.54
Words per Entry	139.4	69.6	114.0	96.7
Syllables per 100 Words	129.5	138.1	131.1	125.8
Words per Sentence	14.0	12.4	14.9	14.5
Percent of Incomplete Sentences	35.8	42.8	28.3	32.4
Negatives per 100 Words	.81	.79	.84	.79
Explosives per 100 Words	19.4	19.0	16.3	18.3
Ego Pronouns per 100 Words	1.97	1.39	1.62	1.59
Solidarity Pronouns per 100 Words	1.88	2.44	2.06	2.64
Detached Pronouns per 100 Words	1.47	1.12	1.41	1.19

(8) Officers tended to use more ego pronouns than enlisted men (p=.10), with the greatest difference between Northern officers (1.97) and Northern enlisted men (1.39).

(9) Enlisted men tended to use more solidarity pronouns than officers (p=.01), with the greatest difference between enlisted Southerners (2.64) and Northern officers (1.88). Note that Northern officers used the most ego pronouns but the least solidarity pronouns, and that enlisted Northerners used the fewest ego pronouns but next to the most solidarity pronouns; as expected, the rates run counter to each other.

(10) Officers tended to use more detached pronouns than enlisted men (p=.10).

The results of the style counts on the letters are shown in Table 17. Again, the two-way analysis of variance test shows the following differences among letter-writers and their levels of statistical significance:

Table 17 Characteristics of Letter Style

Variable	Group averages			
	Northern Officers (N=32)	Northern Enlisted (N=28)	Southern Officers (N=23)	Southern Enlisted (N=24)
Mean Words per Letter	542.3	637.2	577.9	426.4
Syllables per 100 Words	132.1	125.9	131.2	126.9
Words per sentence	20.8	20.1	21.0	15.7
Percent of Incomplete Sentences	4.1	5.9	2.5	3.5
Negatives per 100 Words	1.4	1.8	1.8	1.5
Explosives per 100 Words	18.3	17.9	17.4	18.5
Ego Pronouns per 100 Words	3.67	4.34	4.68	5.70
Solidarity Pronouns per 100 Words	2.39	2.91	2.25	2.35
Detached Pronouns per 100 Words	2.82	3.49	4.07	4.53

(1) The differences on mean words per letter were not statistically significant.

(2) Officers tended to use more syllables per 100 words than enlisted men (p=.10), with the greatest difference between Northern officers (132.1 syllables) and enlisted Northerners (125.9 syllables).

(3) Officers tended to use more words per sentence in their letters than enlisted men (p=.10), with the greatest differences between Southern officers (21.0) and enlisted Southerners (15.7).

(4) Northerners tended to write more incomplete sentences than Southerners (p=.10), with the greatest difference between enlisted Northerners (5.9%) and Southern officers (2.5%).

(5) The differences on the use of negative words in the letters are not statistically significant.

(6) There were no statistically significant differences among the letter-writers on the use of initial explosive sounds.

(7) There were two significant relationships on ego pronouns: Southerners tended to use them more than Northerners (p=.01), and

enlisted men more than officers (p=.05), with the greatest differences between enlisted Southerners (5.70) and Northern officers (3.67).

(8) There were no significant differences among the letter-writers on the use of solidarity pronouns.

(9) Southerners tended to use detached pronouns more often than Northerners (p=.01), with the greatest difference occurring between enlisted Southerners (4.53) and Northern officers (2.82).

The above findings from both studies of letters and diaries can be presented as follows:

(1) Northerners were more methodical than Southerners, in the sense that they were more likely to keep their diaries up-to-date. Southern officers were least methodical.

(2) Officers were more expressive and verbose than enlisted men, in the sense that they wrote longer diary entries. Northern enlisted men were most laconic in that respect.

(3) Officers were more verbose than enlisted men, in the sense that they used longer words in their letters; enlisted Northerners used the shortest words in their letters. However, in the diaries there were no significant differences.

(4) Southern officers were the most verbose, in the sense that they wrote the longest sentences in both their diaries and letters.

(5) Enlisted Northerners were the most laconic, in the sense that they wrote incomplete sentences most often in both their diaries and letters. Southern officers were the most verbose, in the sense that they wrote complete sentences most often in both their diaries and letters.

Those are the strongest findings from both letters and diaries without contradictions; the other findings were either not clear or not significant. The results on pronoun usage are particularly confusing when we compare diaries with letters; for example, Northern officers tended to write about themselves as individuals in their diaries, but not in their letters. Enlisted Southerners wrote about themselves as individuals in their letters, but they spoke of themselves as members of groups in their diaries. But, in general, our assumption about the relationship between expressiveness of emotion and expressiveness in writing is supported by this research on the personal documents of Civil War soldiers: Southern officers were most expressive, and enlisted Northerners were least expressive.

The possibility remains that those differences in writing style could reflect differences in education rather than personality. There were 14

Southern officers writing diaries who were college students, graduates, or professional men, while there were only 7 enlisted Northerners of comparable education writing diaries. The educational differences among letter-writers were even greater: 23 Southern officers were college men or professionals, while only 4 enlisted Northerners were classified that way. In order to check that possibility, let us look closely at that total of 11 enlisted Northerners who were "college" or "professional." We will examine their rates of incomplete sentences, one of the variables with the clearest and most persuasive results. The average rate of incomplete sentences written by enlisted Northern diarists was 42.8%. Of the 7 enlisted Northern diarists who were college or professional men, 3 of them wrote more incomplete sentences than that (62.7%, 45.9%, 60.0%), and 4 of them wrote fewer than that (20.4%, 17.5%, 27.9%, 16.8%). The average for the 7 was 35.9%, which is still higher than the average for all Southern officers writing diaries, 28.3%. The average rate of incomplete sentences among all enlisted Northern letter-writers was 5.9%. Of the 4 who were college or professional men, 2 had higher rates of incomplete sentences (6.9%, 21.4%), and the other 2 men did not have their rates counted because of coding errors, so those figures did not affect the statistics or the comparisons. The rate of incomplete sentences for all Southern officers writing letters was 2.5%. The point is that enlisted Northerners who were highly educated were not more likely to write complete sentences than less-educated enlisted Northerners. We can conclude that the Northerners' laconic, less expressive style was tied to their personality, not their education. This is not to say that education had absolutely no effect on core value expressiveness, character value expressiveness, or style of expressiveness. But simply being an enlisted Northerner or a Southern officer seems to have had the greatest effect on written expressiveness in general.

Another statistical test, discriminant analysis, further shows that each group of soldiers wrote stylistically unique personal documents. The test examines all the comparable style characteristics of a soldier's diary or letter, compares them with the characteristics of all four groups' diaries or letters, and then predicts the probable group membership of the soldier. The results of this procedure are presented in Table 18. If there were no stylistic differences whatsoever among the four groups' personal documents, then all the results in Table 18 would be 25%—the test would be as likely to predict incorrectly as correctly. However, the discriminant analysis shows that in every group the percentage of the correct prediction is higher than each incorrect prediction (though the chance of placing a soldier into a wrong group is higher than the chance of placing him into the right group). Chi-square analysis of the data in Table 18 shows that the

Table 18 Discriminant Analysis of the Style Characteristics of
          Diaries and Letters Combined

Actual Group	Predicted Group Membership (%)			
	Northern Officers (N=85)	Northern Enlisted (N=90)	Southern Officers (N=58)	Southern Enlisted (N=59)
Northern Officers	35.3	22.4	21.2	21.2
Northern Enlisted	16.7	43.3	18.9	21.1
Southern Officers	17.2	22.4	41.4	19.0
Southern Enlisted	22.0	23.7	18.6	35.6

pattern of results from discriminant analysis is statistically significant at the .001 level. In other words, merely by looking at certain style characteristics of a Civil War diary or letter, one has a better than random chance of identifying what type of soldier wrote that document. One has the best chance of identifying the documents of enlisted Northerners and Southern officers. If the key word rates were included as a style characteristic in the discriminant analysis, no doubt the efficiency of the test would be improved, especially its ability to identify correctly the documents of those two types of soldiers.

Considering these results, the reader might wonder again if all the book's results are simply an artifact of the qualities, specifically the lengths, of the soldiers' personal documents. Many precautions were taken in the methodology in order to remove such doubts; nevertheless, the point bears repetition: soldiers did not simply write long diaries and letters or short ones and thus appear more or less expressive. Rather, their expressive dispositions were such that they tended to write longer or shorter personal documents. No personal document has an existence by itself, no document is "accidentally" one rate of characteristics or another: the personal document, it stands to reason, is the revealing creation of a writer. Moreover, this research would have done violence to the evidence if it had only compared personal documents of similar styles and lengths. The different distributions of the styles and lengths of the four groups' documents in this study appear to be a true reflection of those groups' distributions in the real historical world, because this study was based on all the published personal documents which could reasonably be obtained during its execution. But certainly these results should be tested and either confirmed or rejected by another study based on hundreds of *un*published diaries and letters (which, of course, would still be a "biased" sample of the universe of all Americans).

While content analyses of a handful of historical speeches and public documents are quite common, comparative analysis of a mass of historical personal documents is a rare method of research, and stylistic analysis of historical personal documents has never been done before in national character studies. These methods have permitted us to offer systematic and general (if tentative and controversial) answers to some classical but still pressing questions about the nature of the Old South and the Old North. If some of these answers have been stated before by more traditional historians using more conventional methods, that is to be expected and not regretted, since almost every reasonable answer to those classical questions is already on the books.

5 The Experience of Character

To generalize is to be an idiot. To particularize is alone distinction of merit.

William Blake

In this collective study of character, we cannot go into all the details of a single man's moral life. But we should observe men's moral experiences with at least more "fine tuning" than statistics and generalizations have allowed so far, for it is not enough just to describe the theory of character and tabulate its expressions.

Let us take a particular kind of moral experience that would release a writer's character values and then study it closely. Such an experience would be the death of a good man, and the release would come in his surviving companion's letter of condolence to the family. In these letters soldiers would be more likely than ever to describe a man's ethical qualities, whether they were fact or fiction. Indeed, there may not be any document dealing more intensely with character ideals than a condolence letter, the written remains of the ultimate personal event.

It is remarkable that most of the published letters of condolence were written by Southerners. The coders examined 162 sets of published Civil War letters written by Northerners, each set containing from one to several dozen letters, and found only 2 letters of condolence. Then they examined 136 sets of published Civil War letters written by Southerners and found 30 letters of condolence.

It could be concluded that Southern condolence letters are printed more often simply because editors are more interested in them. But that conclusion is doubtful, because letters of condolence are almost never published separately. They occur as the last letter, written by someone else, in a collection of letters written by the deceased. Hence, the condolence letter was published not because it was interesting by itself, but because the victim's whole series of letters was considered worth publishing. Finding so many Southern ones could be judged as either sheer chance or as evidence that Southerners were much more likely to write these messages full of sentiment and appreciation for character. The latter explanation is more convincing: Southerners wrote condolence letters more often because they were more emotionally expressive and more concerned with character than Northerners.

There are general characteristics among the thirty Southern letters.[1] Five types of persons were likely to send condolences from the field on the death of a soldier: commanding officers, chaplains, nurses, comrades, and relatives in uniform. Only the last two usually knew the dead man's biography and family, allowing them to write familiarly. Letters from commanders and chaplains tended to be the most formal, although they could be just as sentimental and intense as those written by nurses, comrades, and relatives. The addressee of the letter would most often be the dead man's wife, mother, or whole family, but rarely the father alone.

Nearly all the writers were apt to begin their letters by expressing their "deep regret" that it was their "painful duty" to inform the kin of the man's death. The announcement of the death would follow, sometimes expressed in the mannered phrase "he is no more." Many of the writers would also say at first that "words fail" them, or "I cannot express my feelings."

The author next seemed likely to give the presentable details of the soldier's death when these were known to him (if he did not explain them, kin sometimes wrote back and asked for details). This is the part of the letter most likely to contain dramatic poses—not that the descriptions of dying appear falsified, though some, no doubt, were inaccurate, censored, or embellished. Many of the men may have died exactly as reported, actually "posing" so dramatically. The point is that the event was usually so stylized by the victim, the reporter, or both. Such was Southern culture, which is one of the larger messages of the letters. For example, soldiers were reported in this manner to have been shot in the head and killed instantly:

> ... Albert was sighting his gun ... and while he was as calm, as cool, and, at the same time, as cheerful as ever even in the midst of a shower of balls, one of them struck him over the left eyebrow & passed thru' his head. He fell into the arms of his friend, Wilkinson, breathed one sigh, and all was over with as pure and noble a son as was ever granted to earthly parents. [letter of Rev. Philip Slater Fall]

If dying from wounds or disease, the victims were often reported to have lingered for a few days, waiting calmly, peacefully, and prayerfully, ready and willing to die, then finally "falling asleep."

Their self-control was continually stressed, and the metaphor of sleep was very common. It was also usual to say that everything possible had been done for the man, that others sat with him, that he was "happy to die," and that he was "sensible," meaning that he knew he was doomed. Similarly, some men were said to have had "presentiments" of their death before they were struck down. The letters would indicate that these men did not "rage against the dying of the light," as Dylan Thomas later urged; instead, they were portrayed as being graceful, giving final instructions to their attendants. For example:

> He was very calm—& serious—& when he fell it was with as calm a smile as if he was sinking into a placid slumber. [letter of John S. Wise]

> This evening at 3 Oclock your son fell asleep as trust in Christ. his last moments were peaceful. [letter of Kate Brand]

> . . . for myself it was a privilege to sit by his side, & note the gradual departure of a spirit so full of holy assurance & love . . . [letter of Mrs. H. F. Wyche]

Their suffering, in any event, was minimized by the writer. There were very few descriptions of amputations and gore in these thirty letters. When we do find such descriptions they are written in the stark language of Southern "plain folk":

> The ball in his head went in between his eye and ear. I think that it stopped some place near his brain. . . . S. L. McClure had three balls Shot through his body & two through his left arm. His left arm was cut off above the elbow. H. M. Wallace had his wright wrist broke. His left arm was cut off. I think he will die. Sam Elor had his left thigh [hit and] it was cut off. [letter of W. J. O'Daniel]

Something had to be said about the disposition of the corpse, and here there might be more realism, if by realism we mean graphic descriptions of their mortuary science (". . . looked the most natural corpse I ever saw, not the least smell" [letter of William Wakefield Garner]; ". . . we then tide him on a horse and packed him aboute twelve miles . . ." [letter of W. F. Robinson]). The relatives were usually told that the dead man had been buried near camp or where he fell. If the enemy possessed the body, the relatives were told that a decent burial had been pledged by them. They were assured that a marker was placed so that the body could be identified later if it was to

be transported home. But if the distance was very great it was unusual
for the body to be sent home, for it simply decayed too quickly. As one
soldier wrote to a father:

> ... we found decomposition had taken place to such an extent
> that it would have been useless to have attempted to carry him
> home ... knowing it would be no gratification for their friends
> to see them in the condition they would be in by that time,
> besides I think they would have been so offensive that they
> would have been compelled to burry them on the road. In fact
> Buchan had decayed so much that it was utterly impossible for
> anyone to recognize him ... I never saw decomposition
> proceed as rapidly in my life. [letter of M. B. Locke]

The trouble, he said, was with the zinc coffins, which were not air-
tight. Perhaps this author wrote with so much candor because the
father of the victim was a physician; nevertheless, even if dying was
romanticized and pain glossed over, there was still a strong popular
interest in the pathology and physiology of death in the mid-nineteenth
century.

There were other practical matters. The authors of condolences,
especially if they were comrades or relatives of the victims, were likely
to send home his relics, most commonly his ring or a lock of hair. The
amount of money the deceased had in his pockets was noted, and the
author would promise to send that home by mail or messenger.
Otherwise, no one spoke of military souvenirs.

Nearly all letters honored the character and sociability of the dead
soldier. It was often said that he would be missed "more than any
other," or that he was "universally loved," or that he was the "favorite"
of his peers. How the man fit in was important to everyone, especially
if he was an ordinary soldier in the ranks. His religious conduct would
be described in such phrases as "tell his mother that he died a
Christian," there was "no finer Christian," he had "pious Christian
deportment," and he died "as a Christian should." His embodiment of
the military virtues was brought out, as one would expect in these sorts
of letters: he always died "bravely" (emphasized also for those who died
of disease), he was a "true patriot," "calm" again, "cool," and
"gallant." Here are some complete examples:

> ... I never heard him utter an oath or do anything that was not
> becoming a christian man ... Bev was a noble-manly boy;
> high-minded, honorable, and a christian & had one of the best
> tempers I ever saw—He died at his post fighting gallantly for
> his country's cause ... [letter of John S. Wise]

> His manly form, his brave and noble bearing his stubborn bravery are all gone . . . Mrs. Johnson your husband was the bravest of the brave—the noblest among the noble minded. His was a soul that brooked no oppression that suffered no insult—that always sympathised with the weak. We shall not again see any like him. [letter of W. H. D. Carrington]

> Captain Brainard, one of the most honest and gallant men I ever knew, ever deported himself as a Gentleman and a Soldier. . . . Noble and manly in bearing, brave, honest, reliable and true he challenged the admiration of all who knew him. Strict in discipline . . . he was unsurpassed as an officer by any in the Confederate army of his age. [letter of W. C. Oats]

> His fall has cast a gloom over the stern features of our entire command, and while we deeply deplore his loss, we are consoled with the reflection that no better Christian, no finer patriot, nor braver man, ever yielded his life more nobly, nor in a more righteous cause. . . . he had acted with so much calmness and gallantry . . . [letter of C. K. Holman]

Perhaps the most effective way to abbreviate and still communicate all this kind of praise was Kate Brand's simple remark: "I found him a gentleman." The letters are laced with the five key character terms we found earlier, and they emphasize the control of emotion, both its appropriate restraint and release.

The soldiers may have lived up to these terms and they may not have; we can be sure there was neither perfect hypocrisy nor perfect integrity. The point is, these were the standards for behavior, and as standards well known they were bound to have some influence on behavior.

There was very little bitterness or strident ideology in these letters, no doubt because they were meant to comfort rather than provoke people. A writer might say that the man had died in a "righteous cause," or perhaps that "liberty and independence" were the man's goals, but nothing more specific than that. Only one writer had real rancor:

> Let every Southern mother teach their children to hate & detest the name Yankee until the name & race shall become extirpated. [letter of W. H. D. Carrington]

On the other hand, no one spoke of concord between the sections either. The letters simply had their own limited, private purposes, with no room for politics.

Near the end of the letters, when the authors spoke directly to the soldiers' wives or mothers, they sometimes almost commanded the women to take the correct attitude. "Do not grieve too much," they wrote, "you must bare it the best you can" [letter of C. Dicken], "Do not take it No harder than you Can help" [letter of I. G. Patten], or "you must look up to God" [letter of W. H. D. Carrington]. The authors must have thought the women fragile, but perhaps they were unconsciously commanding themselves as well, screwing up their courage for the rest of the campaigns.

Even though some authors were emphasizing the solemnity of their dying comrades or urging the survivors also to discipline themselves, still other authors were confessing, with a flourish, the intensity of their own responses to death: "With tears in my eyes and great emotion I am sitting down to write these lines" [letter of Ansel Sterne]; "Many may shed hot tears over his dear body—But none more than your sympathizing friend" [letter of John S. Wise]; "I feel discomfited and exceedingly gloomy—even reckless and miserable" [letter of W. C. Oats]. Again, not only in the description of the victim's conduct and character, but in the writer's self-descriptions we see the restraint and release of emotion most dramatically.

Finally, the authors of letters of condolence would remind the surviving kin of heaven, the better existence it ought to be, and the promise of everyone meeting there in the end. This advice was not just trivial convention, for we know that soldiers and survivors were often quite religious and serious about eternity. A common phrase here was "God grant that our loss will be his eternal gain."

Every culture develops some method or ritual, elaborate or not, for expressing sympathy after a death for the sake of those left living. These letters demonstrate how that ritual was perfected by the Confederate side in the Civil War, in keeping with Southerners' social character.

6 The Culture and Personality of Character

It would seem that men employ two very distinct methods in the judgment which they pass upon the actions of their fellow men; at one time they judge them by those simple notions of right and wrong which are diffused all over the world; at another they appraise them by a few very special rules which belong exclusively to some particular age and country.

Alexis de Tocqueville

This chapter seeks a general explanation of the national character in the Middle Period of American history, employing some new and old approaches to the study of culture and personality. Specifically, this chapter asks why Civil War soldiers became "goodmen"—why they became so concerned with character—and how they did so—what things they did to themselves and others as they became goodmen. This final chapter also seeks to explain the soldiers' different styles of expressing goodness.

The analysis in this chapter makes use of a theoretical model that helps to clarify the relationship between men and their moral thought and experience. In a fascinating and continuing set of cross-cultural studies in psychological anthropology, John W. M. Whiting, Beatrice Whiting, and their associates have used the following model (Fig. 1). It is, so far, the most promising general plan for "psycho-cultural" research. It cannot, by itself, settle the arguments over the nature of Victorian American character, but at least it may help settle the terms of the arguments.[1]

The Whiting model uses anthropological, historical, and ecological perspectives in the Environment and History boxes, and sociological and economic concepts in the Maintenance Systems box. The Child's Learning Environment box uses learning theory, and the Individual Adult box implies an eclectic theory of personality and behavior. The

Fig. 1 The Whiting Model for Psycho-Cultural Research

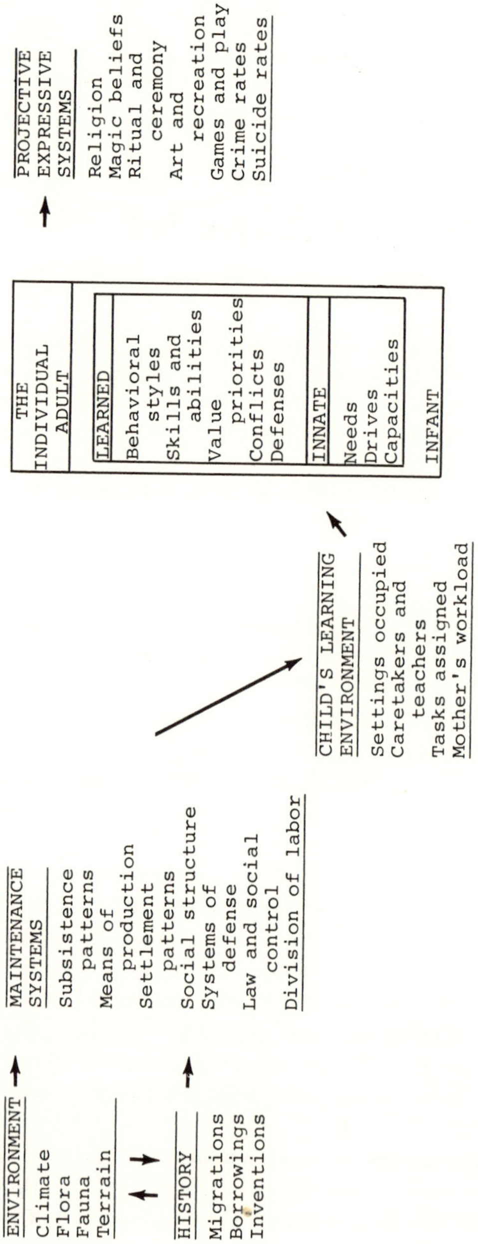

ENVIRONMENT
Climate
Flora
Fauna
Terrain

HISTORY
Migrations
Borrowings
Inventions

MAINTENANCE
SYSTEMS
Subsistence
    patterns
Means of
    production
Settlement
    patterns
Social structure
Systems of
    defense
Law and social
    control
Division of labor

CHILD'S LEARNING
ENVIRONMENT
Settings occupied
Caretakers and
    teachers
Tasks assigned
Mother's workload

THE
INDIVIDUAL
ADULT

LEARNED
Behavioral
    styles
Skills and
    abilities
Value
    priorities
Conflicts
Defenses

INNATE
Needs
Drives
Capacities

INFANT

PROJECTIVE
EXPRESSIVE
SYSTEMS
Religion
Magic beliefs
Ritual and
    ceremony
Art and
    recreation
Games and play
Crime rates
Suicide rates

Projective-Expressive Systems box applies theories from psychoanalysis and folklore. The model has a deterministic flow, but there is a "bottleneck" at the individual: it recognizes that only a person can receive, interpret, and express all the sociocultural forces which press and pull on him. From the humanist's point of view, however, the Individual Adult box still lacks a place for "intellect"; from the determinist's point of view, "intellect," if included, would be labeled as "world view" and placed in the Projective-Expressive Systems box. The model moves from left to right, but there can be dynamic interaction among its parts—cultural expressions and projections may affect maintenance systems, individuals may change the child's learning environment, and so forth.

The Whiting model provides a useful framework for the discussion of results which follows. Each of the three main areas of investigation corresponds to components within the model; that is, why the soldiers become goodmen is tied to Environment, History, and Maintenance Systems; how they became goodmen involves the Child's Learning Environment and the Individual; and the effects of their becoming goodmen are reflected in the Maintenance and Projective-Expressive Systems.

A basic answer to the first question, why the soldiers became goodmen, can be found in a cross-cultural study by Alvin Gouldner and Richard Peterson, *Notes on Technology and the Moral Order.*[2] They applied the statistical technique of factor analysis to masses of ethnographic data on pre-industrial societies that are recorded in the Human Relations Area Files (HRAF). The main question they sought to answer was this: "Is the moral order of a people a result of the techniques by which it gains a livelihood; or is the ethos the determining factor of the character of the total culture?"[3] They concluded that technology was most important, but that ethos was a "close second" (ethos defined as the dominant value system of a culture, or the integrated emotional configuration of its people). Their materialist conclusion suggests that explaining the origins of the Victorian American moral order, and especially the morals of soldiers of the period, can best be accomplished by first looking at the nature of farming and small enterprises, to see how the objective requirements of those occupations influenced group personality and the rules of proper behavior. Gouldner and Peterson say that "Our evidence suggests that the higher the level of technology, the higher the degree of demanded impulse control or Apollonianism."[4] The American farmers, businessmen, and craftsmen of the nineteenth century match or exceed, with their technologies, the most complex technologies represented in the HRAF sample. Thus, the Americans' heavy emphasis on impulse control in their moral order is to be expected.

The subsistence strategies of Victorian Americans are indeed likely to have given rise to, or at least reinforced, strongly held cultural values regarding control and restraint. Men of the period had to discipline themselves to concentrate on learning complex crafts and skills. They had to handle money wisely and discharge just debts promptly. If they "ran their own shop," then they, in effect, paid themselves the wage due for their own labor and nothing more. Every personal failure or episode of laziness would cost them. They tended to live by tighter schedules than the gross phases of the moon. When the crop was ready, they picked it promptly or it rotted. If they made the customer's boots well, they might get to make him another pair. These Americans were directly responsible for their own subsistence—they could not pluck food off trees when they were hungry or trust it would be distributed to them freely by a chief. This is not to say that independent, semi-modern farmers and entrepreneurs wanted no assistance from their government—indeed, they demanded help when they thought they needed it—but the emotional control required by agriculture and petty capitalism, comparatively severe and exacting, was a more important contribution to their value system.

Another pertinent result comes from this anthropological research. In relatively high technology, according to Gouldner and Peterson, "There is a heightening of the sense of self and a new spirit of individuality. . . . The discriminating organism develops a sense of or belief in its own power."[5] Hence, the presence of the core values of Individualism, Progress, Achievement, Materialism, Work, Freedom, Equality, and Efficiency is to be expected in Victorian society, for all those stem from a sufficient sense of self-confidence.

This Apollonianism has costs, however:

> Since Apollonianism is associated with technology, and the latter with growing social tensions, it can scarcely be expected that Apollonianism will be associated with friction-free social relations. Indeed, to the extent that impulse control required by Apollonianism induces cumulative frustrations, Apollonianism itself may be a source of aggression. Impulse control mechanisms may, therefore, create some work for themselves, heightening certain of the very impulses that it is their business to control.[6]

That remark helps to explain the cultural expressions of emotional conflict that were present in the dynamics of the character model itself—as in the children's reader which told them they had to be well-behaved and stifle their anger, and the story in which boys were told they had to be both "gentle" and "manly."

However, caution must be exercised in using Gouldner and Peterson's work to explain nineteenth-century American Apollonianism, because this theory might just as easily be used to prove that there should have been Apollonianism in the seventeenth, eighteenth, and twentieth centuries in America and nearly everywhere else in the Western world, since peoples living in those times and places also possessed relatively high technology. If this theory is to be used to explain our data, the special strength of impulse control in the nineteenth century must be accounted for. Gouldner and Peterson have laid the foundation for this explanation in their statement that the "ethos" of a culture was an almost equally powerful force in producing the moral order. Thus, the Victorian ethos, as expressed in dominant core and character values, was combined with the effects of technology to produce the unique moral order that we find our soldiers following. In sum, they were thinking, feeling, and acting as Max Weber said Protestant Capitalists should logically be expected to think, feel, and act.

How did the soldiers become goodmen? One wishes it were possible to give a comprehensive and scientific account of the precise relationship between modes of historical child-rearing and the resulting adult personalities that have been found here, but so far that account evades historians. However, some rough estimates of the relationship are possible.

Recognizing that group personalities may change significantly over time, one must be very cautious about using research on modern parents and children to explain historical parents and children. But this does not preclude a few reasonable extrapolations. In a review of recent research Wesley Becker offers a summary (Fig. 2) of the consequences of different kinds of parental discipline.[7] As Becker's model shows, restrictiveness tends to produce inhibited behaviors, while permissiveness tends to produce uninhibited behaviors.[8] When restrictiveness is combined with warmth, "good" children, in the traditional sense, are the result. They obey rules and they enforce them, especially if they are boys.[9]

Still another variable in parental behavior can be seen in the differing results of "love-oriented" and "power-assertive" techniques of discipline.[10] The first technique tends to produce children with "internalized reactions to transgressions (feelings of guilt, self-responsibility, confession) and with nonaggressive or cooperative social relations."[11] "Love-oriented" discipline may be expressed in two ways: in its positive form parents use praise and reward; in its negative form they withdraw love—the first tactic being more effective. The second technique, power assertion, which is usually manifested in physical punishment but can also be manifested in verbal aggression,

Fig. 2   Becker's Summary of the Interactive Consequences of
         Different Types of Discipline

	RESTRICTIVENESS	PERMISSIVENESS
WARMTH	Submissive, dependent polite, neat, obedient Minimal aggression Maximum rule enforcement (boys) Dependent, not friendly, not creative Maximal compliance	Active, socially outgoing, creative, successfully aggressive Minimal rule enforcement Facilitates adult role taking Minimal self-aggression Independent, friendly, creative, low projective hostility
HOSTILITY	"Neurotic" problems More quarreling and shyness with peers Socially withdrawn Low in adult role taking Maximal self-aggression (boys)	Delinquency Noncompliance Maximal aggression

tends to "correlate with externalized reactions to transgression (fear of punishment, projected hostility), and with non-cooperative, aggressive behaviors."[12]

If one could apply these leads provided by modern research[13] to a reliable body of systematic data on nineteenth-century child-rearing practices, it would then be possible to predict the likely outcomes of those practices. Unfortunately, very little is known about the actual practices of the time; most of what is known derives from reading old advice manuals on child-rearing, and those manuals may not have reflected the actual behavior of parents.[14] However, good studies of that advice do exist,[15] and there is a common theme in the descriptions they provide: during the mid-nineteenth century, child-rearing was probably characterized by a combination of paternal strictness and maternal warmth, with mothers being most influential in early childhood and fathers in later childhood. One should be uneasy with that generalization, for it says nothing about changing styles of discipline, or variation by region and social class, by age and religion of the parents, by birth order, sex, and innate disposition of the child, by family size and composition, or by fathers' occupations. Nor is there information here on variation from city to farmstead, or simple variation from family to family. Nevertheless, this generalization may be adequate for a simple sketch of an explanation.

Since Victorian children were probably raised with strictness and warmth, it is likely that they tended to be emotionally inhibited, obedient, "rule-enforcing," and overtly nonaggressive. If the tactics of discipline were "love-oriented," boys might be expected to have had strong consciences besides. If the tactics were based on "power-assertion," then one might expect fear of punishment and more aggressiveness, but there would be obedience in either case.

Researching the tactics of discipline in the past often produces uncertain results. For example, in the Middle Period of the nation's history there was a continuing debate on the appropriateness and effectiveness of spanking, but it is difficult to know whether spanking was the predominant mode or simply a rare but noticeable event. The best guess is that "power-assertion" in that form was decreasing and that obedience was effectively secured by other means, even though the child-rearing could still be called strict. It seems fair to suppose that if warmth in child-rearing were increasing, then the first element in the traditional system to give way would probably be the explicit act of spanking. Furthermore, "power-assertion" may not even have been required very often, since family life and the opportunities for identification with the parents may have been so intense that disobedience itself was relatively rare. This would be the case in families in which members interacted with each other nearly all day and in which parents were consistent and confident in their discipline. The family's integration by virtue of religion would also have made for obedience in children and their high identification with their parents. Thus, we can estimate that the boys tended to have strong consciences.

The next step in this investigation introduces a problem that always attends research on child-rearing and its consequences. If children in the first half of the nineteenth century tended to be raised in the general way we have described, does that necessarily mean that they would have been emotionally inhibited and moralistic when they grew up to be Civil War soldiers? In other words, to what extent does childhood experience determine adult personality? The critique of Freudian theory, especially the writings of Karen Horney, and the further development of Neo-Freudian theory, especially the writings of Erik Erikson, have warned us that the experiences of childhood do not rigidly determine the structure of adult personality.[16] Daniel Levinson's more recent research also emphasizes the personality changes that take place in adulthood.[17] On the other hand, common sense persuades us that some childhood experiences must be lasting: "As the twig is bent, so the tree's inclined." Thus, the question is, what effects of child-rearing are likely to be extinguished, and what effects are likely to persist, even though disguised, in later life? This is a fundamental question, and many references could be adduced to support an answer. But again, this is only a sketch of an explanation.

Our estimate will be that such basic behavioral and emotional dispositions as inhibition and moralism would be lasting and influential in
later life. The expressions of these dispositions would change, of
course, because adults are not simply large children. But the
dispositions would still press on the personalitiy. All the clinical
experience of psychoanalysis supports this contention, and even
experiments in behavior modification show how long "habits" such as
these may last. Moreover, these dispositions would be even more likely
to survive if the culture tends to reinforce rather than oppose them. The
culture in which our soldiers were raised did, indeed, support those
dispositions. There was a direct relationship among restrictiveness in
child-rearing, inhibition in personality, and the theme of moral
control in culture.

Now let us deal with what goodmen did, with the moral culture and
society they were busy maintaining and expressing. American life in
the past was marbled with worry over ungoverned passion. To govern
it was a central principle in the conscious organization of institutions and the unconscious structure of imagination. Consider these
examples of their desire for less desire.

Victorians believed that the economy was a test of morals, and that
poverty was a failing mark. The trouble was, they said, that the poor
could not control their impulses. Rescuing the poor, therefore, meant
teaching them willpower and new morals. Many of the poor believed
this too.[18]

Drunkenness in particular was thought to be the quickest way to
give up family, wealth, and self-control. Indeed, there was much
problem drinking and chronic alcoholism in the nineteenth century.
Also, Victorians knew that hard drinking and violence went together.
Thus, the temperance movement was dedicated to increasing people's
willpower and subduing their impulses.

The theory of impulse control was also expressed in nineteenth-
century politics. Leaders were expected to be moral exemplars then,
subject to harsh judgment not only if they had bad policies, but also if
they had badly controlled lives. The politicians themselves were also
more willing to criticize one another's morals, especially their sexual
sins, than they are today, with the result that mud-slinging then was
considerably messier. Victorian political theory also contains projections of moralism. Americans were supposed to be a "self-governing"
people, committed to "local control" and "limited" government. The
powers of the state, like the impulses of men, had to be restrained.

One of the major perceived threats to political stability was the
"mob," as the ungovernable classes were called. One could not trust the
people to govern or control themselves directly, so there must be
mature, thoughtful, controlled representatives placed between the

people and the exercise of power. Neither could the people be trusted to elect their Senators directly, or even the President. The devices of the Constitution were, besides good protection against tyranny, the embodiment of the theory that political passion was dangerous.

Realizing this affords a new perspective on the causes of the Civil War. Of course, the war was fought to preserve the Union (or to secure independence, in the case of a Southerner), and it could not have happened without the issue of slavery. The war itself was not caused by any theory of impulse control. But consider the psychodynamics of much of the rhetoric about the war. The North said its soldiers had to put an end to the Southern "rebellion," that section's defiance of authority and proper governance. As these Union men would not tolerate the rebellion of their emotions, neither could they tolerate the rebellion of any states: Thomas Kilby Smith, a Northern officer, wrote in a letter, "This war has had its origins in lawless and malignant passion."[19] The "Union"—representing symbolically the balance of the appetites, the stability of the soul, the control gained by securing "one out of many"—had to be restored. Union was an emotional concept as well as a political one. On the other side, the Southerners denied that they were "rebels." To them, it was the "war between the states," for they could not admit to treason, or, deeper still, confess that they wanted to destroy "union." What they fought for, they insisted, was a return to "self-government." They too were worried by the threat of external control; they required internal control. As they watched the number of free states increase, it was not only votes in Congress that concerned them; they feared "losing control" to the North, which would also mean losing control of their slaves.

This last point offers a glimpse of the mind set which underlay the dominant response of the whole country to its aliens—immigrants, Indians, and blacks. Most white Americans felt that the trouble with these peoples, especially the last two, was that they were "savages." It was not only their strange customs which were found unattractive, it was also their imagined personalities. They all tended to be stereotyped, publicly and privately, as irrational, erotic, and ungovernable things.[20] Blacks were deemed to be the figurative slaves of their own passions, and that vulnerability required that they be the actual slaves of proper men who could control them. The Indians had to be "civilized" or contained on reservations, and the immigrants had to be isolated in ghettos or "exiled," in a manner of speaking, to the frontier. In any event, the right people believed they must be rid of them all or restrain them when they became too numerous. To be sure, there were many practical reasons why Americans feared these people—there were rebellions among the slaves and resistance by the Indians whose land was taken over by the settlers, and the immigrants' different ways of speaking and acting made them appear threatening. There were also obvious economic reasons why these stereotypes were convenient to maintain. But the emotional undercurrents interest us most here. Northerners and Southerners hated most in other peoples, and in each other, what they feared most in themselves. Despite the many excellent studies we have of racial stereotyping in the nineteenth century, some central questions remain: how often, and under what circumstances, did the behavior of Afro-Americans correspond with their image, how often did it contradict it, and how often did it fall between those two extremes? Biographies and monographs cannot answer those questions fully, and the present study only takes the position that the whites' image of the blacks reveals more about white personality than black. But we can be certain that there were blacks and whites who saw through the image and treated one another as fellow creatures instead of caricatures. We also know that "practical" considerations could overcome racial stereotyping—the Union put 186,000 blacks in uniform in order to destroy slavery, while the Confederacy actually debated arming slaves in order to defend the "peculiar institution." If there were Abolitionists as well as callous or hypocritical Northerners, if there were Southerners who manumitted their slaves out of conscience as well as petty tyrants who were unspeakably cruel to their "property," if there were passionate Africans who led revolts as well as those who survived by becoming seemingly docile "Sambos," then from a moral point of view (which is hardly irrelevant, even in quantitative history), all Americans have some ancestors of whom they can feel greatly proud and some of whom they might feel quite ashamed, but in any case it is necessary to try to understand them all as "frankly human," in Santayana's phrase.

The anxious qualities in the American character are also revealed by examining the theory and practice of psychiatry in the mid-nineteenth century. Even today psychiatry is part cultural and moral theory, but in the past that tendency was much more pronounced: psychiatry was predominantly cultural and moral theory, mixed with some mistaken biological theory. In the early part of the nineteenth century psychiatrists established a major new diagnostic category, "moral insanity," to go along with mania, melancholia, and dementia, the main disorders of emotion and reason. Dr. John Prichard, an English psychiatrist, first defined it in 1835 as

> a morbid perversion of the natural feelings, affections, inclinations, temper, habits, moral dispositions, and natural impulses, without any remarkable disorder or defect of the intellect or knowing and reasoning faculties, and particularly without any insane illusion or hallucination. . . . The individual is found

to be incapable not of talking or reasoning upon any subject proposed to him, for this he will often do with great shrewdness and volubility, but of conducting himself with decency and propriety in the business of life.[21]

The times demanded so much morality that immorality—losing control of the impulses—had to be called insanity. Every man had to have a "moral sense" or else he was simply not a normal creature.[22] At about this same time, "moral treatment" was invented as a new therapy in psychiatry.[23] This meant "compassionate and understanding treatment of innocent sufferers." In effect, patients were made comfortable. The staff was told to be friendly and to discuss the patients' troubles with them, and patients were given activities to fill their days. Some physicians believed moral treatment was so effective that at first they reported most of their patients were "discharged recovered." Whether they were or not, the point is that during the Middle Period the theory and practice of psychiatry were clear manifestations of the moral enthusiasm of Americans and their anxiety over the loss of control.

Men's images of women were a most interesting screen for their projections. In fact, the whole Victorian system of sex role differences becomes more understandable if we use the dynamics of impulse control to interpret it. Both men and women were supposed to be, in their own ways, honorable, pure, and pious; both had to have their emotions under control. Otherwise there were remarkably opposite expectations for each sex. Men had to be brave and assertive and work for a living, but women had to be submissive, gentle, and domestic.[24] Women were permitted to express more sentiment and emotion; they were hardly complimented for "thinking like a man." In making these assignments, it seems men were unconsciously allowing the opposite sex to display those traits that had to be stored up and hidden in themselves. This was an elaborate form of projection, and the projection was necessary because the men could not tolerate the possibility that they might be effeminate or, God forbid, homosexual. The amount of praise for women's "soft" natures may be directly proportional to the amount of tension men felt as they lived out their own almost passionless contracts.

This leads us to the most blatant cultural expression of the Victorian desire for less desire, namely the rules and practice of sexual conduct. The quickest glance through the health and marriage manuals published in the mid-1800s, and just a little more time spent studying the more subtle public lectures given to young men and women, suggests that most Americans were more upset by sex than by slavery.[25] We underestimate the Victorians if we say they were simply prudish, although they were certainly prudish. Consider the advice they were given by their elders. One of them, Dr. Benjamin Rush, the founder of American psychiatry and a signer of the Declaration of Independence, advised in his famous textbook published in 1812 that to restrain sexual appetite, one must eat "a diet consisting simply of vegetables"; have "long journeys on horseback"; take "a cold bath"; or try "salivating, which diverts morbid excitability from the genitals to the mouth and throat." If those tactics don't work, he wrote, avoid "all dalliance with the female sex . . . I have heard of a clergyman who overcame this appetite by never looking directly in the face of a woman." He also maintained that "certain tones of music have sometimes suddenly relieved a paroxysm of veneral desires," and that "study of any kind, more especially to the mathematics," might take the mind off sex. But finally, noted Dr. Rush, "Dr. Boerhaave says a sudden fit of laughter has sometimes had the same effect."[26] We need not argue that this advice was taken, or that it explains Victorian men's spitting, riding, bathing, shifting eyes, humming, figuring, and laughing. But his advice was deemed plausible by at least a few men who thought their fellows were on the brink and needed the sharpest tricks to hang on. Seventy-five years later, near the end of Victorianism, advice on sexual behavior was just as odd. Dr. Harvey Kellogg's manual, *Plain Facts about Sexual Life* (which sold 300,000 copies between 1880 and 1910), states that weak backs, round shoulders, paralysis, and stooping posture are the signs of youthful masturbators. They could otherwise be identified by the fingernails they had bitten, their extravagant use of spices, their acne, and a cold, moist hand.[27] Advice of this sort came tumbling from the presses after 1830, when most of our soldiers were growing up, and was written mainly by Northeasterners. They, at least, could talk about sex publicly; Southerners would not.

Perhaps the most fundamental evidence regarding Victorian sexual conduct itself occurs in the form of demographic change: the average size of families was decreasing throughout the nineteenth century.[28] In achieving this decline, the major methods of contraception most likely were abstinence and coitus interruptus. The Victorians were probably not reducing the size of their families because they were increasingly afraid of sexual contact, but whatever the cause, the methods required continuing birth control by emotional devices and not mechanical ones. Thus, conception was frustrated, but so were lovers.

Although Victorian culture was laced tight with controls, its people did let loose from time to time. The principle at work here has been stated by Jules Henry: "All cultures offer, through prescribed channels, some outlet for the emotional problems they create; they stipulate, in addition, what emotions may be expressed, by whom, in what quantity, and the circumstances of their expression."[29] Religious practice provided one such channel. Preachers told their flocks to resist secular temptations, but permitted, indeed encouraged them to give in to divine ecstasies. In other words, if men were not supposed to shout in taverns, they were allowed to sing loudly at revival meetings and otherwise relieve their stresses through dramatic conversions. If they could not express anger at their fellow man, in his stead they could despise the Devil and then admire "gentle Jesus, meek and mild." Believers in the well-behaved denominations were suspicious of such revivalism, not only because its intellectual foundations were held faulty, but precisely because the converts acted too wildly. However, some of the intellectuals in the North found their own quite mystical, civilized solution for excessive stress in transcendentalism, with its emphasis on naturalness and spontaneity.

Physical mobility was another channel. If life's demands became too oppressive in the East, men could head West, where they imagined there was more freedom. If Victorians chose not to move West as conventional pioneers, then they might join utopian communities out there. A few of these communities offered emotional release in their radical sexual codes, but personal restraint was still important in Utopia. As one observer put it, "With the right standards of character for both leaders and led, it will be an easy task to multiply communities in all civilized lands."[30] John Humphrey Noyes, sexual radical, birth controller, and founder of the Oneida community, stressed character over all: "Male continence in its essence is self-control, and that is a virtue of universal importance. . . . Nothing less than heart-abandonment to the grace of God, which teaches and gives *temperance in all things* [his emphasis], can ever release us from the old tutelage of suffering."[31]

Men, in sculpting their masculinity, did have one channel open for being gentle, and that was in acting like "gentlemen." (According to Webster's dictionary, the key Southern term "gallant" meant being "magnanimous" to a conquered foe.) This specialized role gave men the ability to accommodate both the "male" and "female" within themselves, as Carl Jung would have put it. The danger here was misplaying the role, having too many effeminate qualities, and thus be called "fops" or "dandies." Clearly, they had to be manly gentlemen. Otherwise, they might earn this sort of insult:

> Sometimes men who held back [from enlisting] even for a little while, as Henry M. Stanley brings out in his *Autobiography*, received gentle reminders in the form of dainty feminine garments sent through the mail.[32]

In spite of these acceptable reprieves from the rule of control, there were plain violations of the rule. The "confession" of William C. Preston is only one mild Southern example. In his reminiscences he said this about his conduct and that of his friends while he worked in a law office:

> The winter was passed in a worse than stationary, it was a retrograde condition. The style of manners amongst the young Virginia gentlemen was that of riot and dissipation and I have always looked back to this period with shame and regret. It was time worse than lost. . . . I am persuaded that I escaped the ordinary fate by a constitutional incapacity for drinking, which is hereditary in my family. No Preston has ever been addicted to that fatal Virginia vice of drunkenness and thus I escaped. We lived fast, were very much addicted to cards, and had an unceasing round of gaiety, in short were persons of "wit and pleasure about town" holding in utter scorn all sedate pursuits or grave occupations. We were roisterers and it is mournful to look back on what became of the members of that winter's society.[33]

Sometimes Civil War soldiers complained about immorality in camp. One called his friend "A very moral young man, which is a considerable rarity in the army."[34] Another wrote home that "Young men who were temperate and moral at home and many of them religious are brought in contact with all the vices of camp life and the good influences of home forgotten. This has a more ruinous effect upon human society than all that are killed upon the battle field."[35] Another said that in the army, "everything corrupt, low, vulgar and debasing in our corrupt nature is rampant."[36] And another said, "I must confess that I had seen but little of the wickedness and depravity of man until I joined the army."[37] Whatever the violations were— gambling, prostitution, drinking, swearing, fighting, crime—Gertrude Himmelfarb's comment about the English Victorians may be applied to their American counterparts: "Even the violations of propriety reinforced the sense of propriety."[38]

If all the Civil War soldiers closely resembled one another, then this general explanation would be completed. But, as has been pointed out, the groups of soldiers were not all alike. Southerners were most expressive, (especially officers) and Northerners were least expressive (especially enlisted men). Also, the Southern officers valued Humanitarianism, Individualism, and Will a great deal more than the enlisted Northerners, and they also used the five key character terms more often than the enlisted Northerners.

There are several ways to resolve this difficulty and still retain the general explanation. First, from Gouldner and Peterson's study it can be argued that Northerners were least expressive (most Apollonian) because their technology was higher than that of the Southerners. Another possible explanation comes from a related study from cross-cultural research in psychological anthropology.[39] Barry, Child, and Bacon have argued that societies with "low accumulation of subsistence goods" will tend to value achievement, self-reliance, and independence—"assertion" their study calls it—whereas societies with "high accumulation of subsistence goods" will be more likely to value obedience, responsibility, and nurturance—their study calls it "compliance." Thus, it could be argued that Northerners, having relatively higher accumulations of goods and higher technologies, would be more compliant and willing to restrain their emotions, while Southerners, having relatively lower accumulations of goods and lower technologies, would be more assertive and willing to express their emotions more readily. They would value individualism and willfulness even more than the bourgeois Northerners.

If those two answers from cross-cultural research are not suitable for regional comparisons in America, there are two others with a more specific applicability: Eugene Genovese's thesis that Northerners were capitalists and Southerners were pre-capitalists, which would explain the differences in the strengths of their impulse control and Apollonianism; and, from Richard Brown's *Modernization*, the argument that the North was more modern than the South, which would also explain the North's greater Apollonianism.[40]

There is a fifth opportunity to explain regional variation, and it deals more concretely and directly with American group personalities and class differences than the other four studies. It comes from Philip Greven's *The Protestant Temperament*, an excellent study of eighteenth-century child-rearing techniques and their consequences.[41] Greven finds three major modes of child-rearing linked with three major modes of religious experience in early America. He calls them Evangelical, Moderate, and Genteel. The Evangelical mode was distinguished by self-suppression and authoritarianism, the Moderate by self-control and respectable moralism, and the Genteel by self-approval and self-assertion. The central tendency which emerged from our general discussion of child-rearing seems to combine Greven's Moderate and Evangelical modes. If these three modes continued to be practiced well into the nineteenth century (and Greven says they were), then the greater expressiveness of Southern officers might be due to their having been raised more often by genteel parents, and the lesser expressiveness of enlisted Northerners might be due to their having been raised more often by evangelical and moderate parents. The other two groups of soldiers, enlisted Southerners and Northern officers, were probably raised in a less readily identifiable mixture of the three modes. (It is also possible that our four samples of soldiers are so constituted in this study that the Southern officers just happen to reflect best the Genteel mode, that the enlisted Northerners just happen to reflect best the Evangelical and Moderate modes, and that the other two groups just happen not to reflect the expression of any particular mode of child-rearing.)

Greven does not directly link child-rearing modes and religious experience with region of the country except in one instance. Indeed, in this instance he lets regional variation override child-rearing variation in explaining degrees of expressiveness. He writes that,

> . . . genteel Southerners often seem to be notably open and at ease with their feelings. . . . The genteel in more northerly regions seem to have been more equable [steady] in their temperaments.[42]

There are no such direct comparisons of Northern moderates and evangelicals with Southern moderates and evangelicals.

Unfortunately, we do not know whether the most powerful variable in Greven's study for explaining emotional expressiveness is child-rearing mode, religious experience, regional experience, or a combination of all three. If we were able to quantify more exactly the distributions of styles of religious experience and modes of child-rearing in the two regions it might be possible to offer a better explanation for variations in emotional expressiveness than either Greven's study or this one do by themselves.

Taken all together, these five opportunities for a solution—the findings from two massive cross-cultural studies, from two large-scale American social histories, and from a historical child-rearing study—help explain, in general, regional variations in emotional expression. But there remains a singular social fact of Southern life which must be discussed in any complete explanation of regional variation. That fact is the relationship between blacks and whites.

Where slave labor was very profitable in the South, the percentage of the whole population which was black was remarkably high. In South Carolina in 1850, 53% of the population was black; in the counties along the Mississippi River in Louisiana and Mississippi, about 70% of the population was black.[43] Blacks were not predominant throughout the South, but they were certainly obvious. Given today's knowledge of anxiety and its production of distortions of visual perception, it seems possible that white Southerners in 1850 might have felt the number of blacks to be even higher than it actually was. As Charles Grier Sellers, Jr., has written, "the essential key to understanding the Old South seems to lie in the area of social psychology."[44]

The Southern white's necessary knowledge of the black may have had many effects on both their personalities. In the confusing tangle of their emotions, they may have borrowed certain traits from one another by accident, envy, or fear. For example, Africans and Englishmen obviously did not arrive in the 1600s with the same fully developed "Southern accents," but by the mid-1800s both races had those utterly distinctive twangs and slurs in their speech. The alliance of black and white ways of speaking in the South shows the subtle strength of the races' emotional and cultural interaction.

After over two hundred years of living next to each other, Southern whites and blacks had thus transformed each other. The Africans had become part Southern American, and the Southern Americans had become part African, but were also still part Englishmen. The white character model was partly English in its celebration of the Gentleman—Southerners did not invent the words "noble" and "gallant." That was their medieval and Cavalier inheritance, adapted to their American experience. But their emphasis on emotional control and their moral literature were mainly American, and their interaction here with blacks produced their "Dionysianism" (the opposite of Apollonianism, stressing emotional release instead of control). In the North, Apollonianism had no competition, but in the South there was the black to oppose it. And the black, according to Cash, was "one of the world's greatest romantics and one of the world's greatest hedonists" (certainly an exaggeration). The black, said Cash, "entered into white man as profoundly as white man entered into Negro—subtly influencing every gesture, every word, every emotion and idea, every attitude."[45] The black showed the white how to release, but thereby he also proved the need for control: as Winthrop Jordan has written, "Above all, the white man had to sustain his feeling of control; in restraining the Negro he was at the same time restraining and reassuring himself."[46]

This ambivalence toward the black led to a Southern character structure that was more intense than the Northern one in two respects—more intensely controlled, and more intensely needing control. This is partly why the character model is summoned more often in the Southern diaries and letters. The model served Southerners with both the chance for restraint and the chance for release; it gave them the opportunity to be both manly and gentle, both ardent and cool. In the Apollonian North it was all much "simpler": just keep control; use a regular "hurrah" when charging the enemy, not that screeching rebel yell. But when the Yankees were similarly provoked—

when they met the Indians, for instance—they would produce their own Northern version of the Dionysian Southerner: the still stoical but violent mountain men and cowboys.

We can offer not as proofs but as demonstrations of this theory some brief examples of emotional control at work in soldiers' documents. The North's effort at sheer control is revealed in Lieutenant John Wilder's rules for his own behavior: "Be impudent but coolly, and abound in cheek," he wrote, and finally, "Never get excited."[47] Union Captain Cyrus Carpenter, writing to his wife about the death of President Lincoln, mourned that now the country would be without his "calm wisdom, his dispassionate mind . . . and his noble Christian character."[48] Union Lieutenant Fred Lockley felt the same way about Lincoln: ". . . he has shown such an impassibility to any human infirmity of temper, rising like a demigod above all angry and senseless invective."[49] Perhaps Henry Adams summarized the Northern condition best when he wrote later in his *Education*, that "Each individual was satisfied to stand alone . . . yet to stand alone is quite natural when one has no passions."[50]

There are also remarks revealing the Southern effort to balance release and restraint. Confederate Major Thomas Rowland described a friend: "Frank, open hearted, generous and impetuous, he is a true type of Southerner and a most agreeable companion."[51] William L. Wilson said of Colonel Mosby, "polite and generous to a conquered foe he always fought with hearty good will and terrible earnestness."[52] William Pendleton wrote, "O how it comforts the soldier's heart to meet with kind treatment. And how it encourages him to be more determined than ever in the discharge of his duty."[53]

Finally, there is one more reason why Northerners and Southerners differed from one another: they probably chose to. Perhaps that existential fact seems out of place in the logic of this study, but it must be included with all the social facts compiled here.

We should not leave this sketch thinking that Americans, depending on their region, were either the most inhibited or the most flamboyant people on the face of the earth, for clearly they were not. Anyone familiar with Ruth Benedict's *Patterns of Culture* will recall that the Pueblo peoples of the Southwest evinced more Apollonian restraint than our enlisted Northerners, the Kwakiutl Indians of the Pacific Northwest more Dionysian exhibitionism than our Southern officers. We know that all cultures must cope with the problem of impulse control, and so discomfort themselves more or less.

Moreover, we need not think that Victorian Americans had especially strange reasons for being so controlled. They had very practical reasons. They all had to grit their teeth through pain, worry through childbirth, and live through epidemics. Their churches were not necessarily a comfort to them, and their labor was not necessarily profitable. Spirited horses might kick them and primitive machines might mangle them. They had to defend their honor among their peers and cope with rowdies in the streets. They needed to be callous enough to kill animals. They watched their fathers and mothers die at home after they had spent years obeying them.

Civil War soldiers had especially good reasons for keeping cool: can we imagine the self-discipline required in facing and charging the barricades in battle after battle? It may have been a relief to be a hidden bushwhacker, presuming you could murder without flinching and giving yourself away. What was in store for a soldier if he were wounded? Not an excellent chance for survival, let alone with all his limbs.

To expect a relaxed, tolerant, spontaneous people to emerge from this milieu is to count on a miracle. In short, they were discontented, but civilized. They had to want to become what they were required to become. Only our arrogance or innocence would allow us to claim that we, in their place, would have done a little better, or that now we do much better. We should have a decent respect for their necessary troubles and their sufficient sanity. To rebuke them would be to rebuke our own past, which we carry with us always, like it or not. Victor Houghton advised us best:

> We still imagine that our frame of mind is as different from that of the Victorians as our clothes, and as obviously superior . . . but our own candor, sincerity, and measured judgment, so far as we possess these virtues more than the Victorians, have been purchased at the loss of some valuable convictions.[54]

Notes

INTRODUCTION

1. This material first appeared in a different form as part of an article; see Michael Barton, "The Civil War Letters of Captain Andrew Lewis and his Daughter," *Western Pennsylvania Historical Magazine*, 60 (1977), 371–390.

2. Samuel Bates, *History of the Pennsylvania Volunteers, 1861–5*, vol. I (Harrisburg, Pa.: B. Singerly, State Printer, 1869), pp. 845–857; Samuel McCartney Jackson, *Diary of General S. M. Jackson for the Year 1862* (Apollo, Pa.: privately printed, 1925), introd.

3. Charles W. Sanders, *The School Reader, Second Book* (Philadelphia: Sower, Barnes, 1861), pp. 77–79.

4. *Confederate First Reader* (Richmond, Va.: Published by George L. Bidgood, 1864), p. 16.

CHAPTER 1

1. Quoted in Kenneth M. Stampp, ed., *The Causes of the Civil War*, rev. ed. (Englewood Cliffs, N. J.: Prentice-Hall, 1965), p. 184.

2. Quoted in Stampp, p. 184.

3. Henry Adams, *The Education of Henry Adams*, ed. Ernest Samuels (1918; rpt. Boston: Houghton Mifflin Riverside Editions, 1973), pp. 100–101.

4. Quoted in William R. Taylor, *Cavalier and Yankee; The Old South and American National Character* (1961; rpt. Garden City: Doubleday Anchor, 1963), p. 217.

5. Ralph Waldo Emerson, *Essays, Second Series*, vol. 3 of *The Complete Works of Ralph Waldo Emerson* (1844; rpt. New York: AMS Press, 1968), p. 97.

6. Quoted in Clement Eaton, *The Mind of the Old South*, rev. ed. (Baton Rouge: Louisiana State University Press, 1967), p. 245, and in Taylor, *Cavalier and Yankee*, pp. 246, 265–266.

7. Quoted in Taylor, p. vii.

8. For other Northern opinions on Southern licentiousness, see Ronald G. Walters, "The Erotic South: Civilization and Sexuality in American Abolitionism," *American Quarterly*, 25 (1973), 177–201.

9. See Thomas J. Pressly, *Americans Interpret Their Civil War* (New York: Free Press, 1962).

10. Allan Nevins, *The Ordeal of the Union*, 2 vols. (New York: Charles Scribner's Sons, 1947), I: pp. viii–x, 532–535; II: 537–544.

11. Eugene Genovese, *The Political Economy of Slavery* (New York: Vintage, 1965), pp. 3, 7, 23, 28, 35.

12. C. Vann Woodward, "The Southern Ethic in a Puritan World," *William and Mary Quarterly*, 25 (1968). See also David Bertelson, *The Lazy South* (New York: Oxford University Press, 1967), on the Southern theory of work, and George B. Tindall, *The Ethnic Southerners* (Baton Rouge: Louisiana State University Press, 1976).

13. Thomas P. Govan, "Americans Below the Potomac," in Charles Grier Sellers, Jr., ed., *The Southerner as American* (1960; rpt. New York: E. P. Dutton, 1966), pp. 19–39.

14. Edmund Morgan, "The Puritan Ethic and the American Revolution," *The William and Mary Quarterly*, 24 (1967), 3–43.

15. Howard Zinn, *The Southern Mystique* (New York: Simon and Schuster Touchstone Book, 1972), pp. 217–218.

16. David Potter, *The South and Sectional Conflict* (Baton Rouge: Louisiana State University Press, 1968), pp. 3, 16.

17. David Potter, *The Impending Crisis, 1848–1861* (New York: Harper and Row, 1976), p. 42.

18. Carl Degler, "The Two Cultures and the Civil War," in Stanley Coben and Lorman Ratner, eds., *The Development of an American Culture* (Englewood Cliffs, N. J.: Prentice-Hall, 1970), pp. 95, 103, 96.

19. Carl Degler, *Place Over Time; The Continuity of Southern Distinctiveness* (Baton Rouge: Louisiana State University Press, 1977), pp. 68, 60.

20. W. J. Cash, *The Mind of the South* (New York: Vintage Books, 1941). See the remarks, simultaneously critical and respectful, in Zinn, pp. 217–263; Woodward, pp. 261–83; Genovese, pp. 137–150; and Joseph L. Morrison, "W. J. Cash: The Summing Up," *South Atlantic Quarterly*, 70 (1971), 477–486.

21. Ibid., p. viii.

22. Ibid., p. 32.

23. Ibid., p. 35.

24. Ibid., p. 45.

25. Ibid., pp. 46–47.

26. Ibid., p. 52.

27. Ibid., pp. 73, 76.

28. Ibid., pp. 75–77.

29. Ibid., pp. 57–60.

30. Ibid., pp. 54–55.

31. John Hope Franklin, *The Militant South* (1956; rpt. Boston: Beacon Paperbacks, 1964), pp. 32–36.

32. Rollin G. Osterweis, *Romanticism and Nationalism in the Old South* (1949; rpt. Baton Rouge: Louisiana State University Press, 1971), pp. 238, 82–102.

33. Another "psychological analysis," thoroughly Freudian, is Earl E. Thorpe, *The Old South: A Psychohistory* (Durham, N. C.: Seeman Printery, 1972). But see John Blassingame's review, "The Planter on the Couch: Earl Thorpe and the Psychodynamics of Slavery," *Journal of Negro History*, 60 (1975), 320–331.

34. Murray Murphey, "An Approach to the Historical Study of National Character," in Melford E. Spiro, ed., *Context and Meaning in Cultural Anthropology* (New York: Free Press, 1965), pp. 144–163. See Stannard's review, "American Historians and the Idea of National Character: Some Problems and Prospects," *American Quarterly*, 23 (1971), 202–220. See also Nancy Pries, "Patterns of Value Emphasis in the Antebellum North" (Diss. Pennsylvania 1972), which has a methodology similar to Murphey's.

35. George Wilson Pierson, "The Obstinate Concept of New England: A Study in Denudation," *New England Quarterly*, 28 (1955), pp. 10, 13–15.

36. David Riesman, with Nathan Glazer and Ruel Denney, *The Lonely Crowd; A Study of the Changing American Character* (New Haven: Yale Universitiy Press, abrid. ed., 1969). See also the collected critical comments in Seymour Martin Lipset and Leo Lowenthal, eds., *Culture and Social Character* (Glencoe, Ill.: Free Press, 1961).

37. Ibid., pp. 13–24, 126, 123.

38. Ibid., p. 32.

39. Richard D. Brown, *Modernization; The Transformation of American Life, 1600–1865* (New York: Hill and Wang, 1976), pp. 146–148.

40. Edward Pessen, *Jacksonian America; Society, Personality, and Politics* (Homewood, Ill.: Dorsey Press, 1969), pp. 5-34.

41. Bell Wiley, "Johnny Reb and Billy Yank Compared," *American History Illustrated*, 3 (1968), 4-9, 44-47.

42. Ibid., p. 47.

43. Ibid., p. 47.

44. Bell Wiley, *The Life of Billy Yank* (Indianapolis: Bobbs-Merrill, 1952), and *The Life of Johnny Reb* (Indianapolis: Bobbs-Merrill, 1943), contain more comparisons.

45. David Donald, "The Confederate as a Fighting Man," in Charles Grier Sellers, Jr., ed., *The Southerner as American* (1960; rpt. New York: E. P. Dutton, 1966), p. 73.

46. Ibid., pp. 80, 87.

47. Ibid., p. 85.

48. Ibid., pp. 88, 77, 73, 86. There are other popular, qualitative studies, some of which make too much of too little evidence. See Fred A. Shannon, "The Life of the Common Soldier in the Union Army, 1861-1865," *Mississippi Valley Historical Review*, 13, (1927), 465-482; and Coman Leavenworth, "Letters from the Field: The Civil War at First Hand," *Columbia Library Columns*, 13 (February, 1964), 3-15.

49. Pete Maslowski, "A Study of Morale in Civil War Soldiers," *Military Affairs*, 34 (1970), 122-126.

50. William R. Taylor, *Cavalier and Yankee; The Old South and American National Character* (1961; rpt. Garden City: Anchor Books, 1963), p. xxi.

51. Ibid., p. 87.

52. Ibid., p. 102.

53. Ibid., p. 217.

54. Ibid., pp. 230, 231.

55. Ibid., p. xvi.

56. Ibid., pp. 312-313.

57. Ibid., p. xxii.

CHAPTER 2

1. Robin M. Williams, Jr., *American Society; A Sociological Interpretation*, 3rd ed. (New York: Knopf, 1970), pp. 438-504.

2. The sources for all the statistical tests used throughout the book are Hubert M. Blalock, Jr., *Social Statistics*, rev. 2nd ed. (New York: McGraw-Hill, 1979); Sidney Siegel, *Non-Parametric Statistics for the Behavioral Sciences* (New York: McGraw-Hill, 1956); Jum C. Nunnally, *Psychometric Theory*, 2nd ed. (New York: McGraw-Hill, 1978); and Norman H. Nie, C. Hadlai Hull, Jean G. Jenkins, Karin Steinbrenner, and Dale H. Bent, *SPSS; Statistical Package for the Social Sciences*, 2nd ed. (New York: McGraw-Hill, 1975).

CHAPTER 3

1. Noah Webster, *An American Dictionary of the English Language*, rev. and enlarged by Chauncey A. Goodrich (Springfield, Mass.: George and Charles Merriam, 1851).

2. A fine study of the social meaning of Webster's meanings is Richard M. Rollins, "Words as Social Control: Noah Webster and the Creation of the *American Dictionary*," *American Quarterly*, 28 (1976), 415-430. At this writing, Rollins's book on

Webster is about to be published (*The Long Journey of Noah Webster*, University of Pennsylvania Press, forthcoming, 1980). In the article Rollins emphasizes that Webster's main purpose in producing the dictionary was to re-establish conservative morals in the face of what he perceived as increasing social disorganization in the early part of the nineteenth century. There is no need here to argue with this interpretation unless Rollins would also claim that Webster's morals were out of step with the writings of other prominent moralists. My conclusion is that, no matter what their cause, the lexicographer's theories were certainly in step with those of other moralists who were writing college textbooks on moral philosophy, giving public lectures, and instructing children in the nineteenth century. They all insisted on impulse control. See also D. H. Meyer, *The Instructed Conscience: The Shaping of the American National Ethic* (Philadelphia: University of Pennsylvania Press, 1974).

CHAPTER 4

1. M. Lorenz and S. Cobb, "Language Patterns in Psychotic and Psychoneurotic Subjects," *A.M.A. Archives of Neurology and Psychiatry*, 72 (1954), 665–673, cited in Harold J. Vetter, *Language Behavior and Psychopathology* (Chicago: Rand McNally, 1969), pp. 106–107. See also, Edward Sapir, "Speech as a Personality Trait," *American Journal of Sociology*, 32 (1927), 892–905.
2. Irwin A. Berg, "Word Choice in the Interview and Personal Adjustment," *Journal of Counseling Psychology*, 5 (1958), 130–135.
3. Helen Fairbanks, "The Quantitative Differentiation of Samples of Spoken Language," *Psychological Monographs*, 56 (1944), 19–38; Mary Bachman Mann, "The Quantitative Differentiation of Samples of Written Language," *Psychological Monographs*, 56 (1944), 41–74.
4. Berg, p. 131.
5. Fillmore H. Sanford, "Speech and Personality," *Psychological Bulletin*, 39 (1942), 827.

CHAPTER 5

1. The analysis of condolence letters first appeared in a slightly different form as an article; see Michael Barton, "Painful Duties: Art, Character, and Culture in Confederate Letters of Condolence," *Southern Quarterly*, 17 (1979), 123–134.
Another study of consolation literature in general is Ann Douglas's "Heaven Our Home: Consolation Literature in the Northern United States, 1838–1880," *American Quarterly*, 26 (1974), 496–515.
Two of my former students, Patricia Faust and Carol Strait, helped prepare the materials for this chapter and I am grateful for their meticulousness. The letters of condolence we used are: Joseph W. Murphy to Harriet H. Strayhorn, "Letters of Thomas Jackson Strayhorn," ed. Henry McGilbert Wagstaff, *North Carolina Historical Review*, 13 (1936), 334; William Wakefield Garner to Elvira Ellington, "Letters of an Arkansas Confederate Soldier," ed. D. D. McBrien, *Arkansas Historical Quarterly*, 2 (1943), 61; Dabny H. Maury to Mrs. William P. Rogers, "The Diary and Letters of William P. Rogers, 1846–1862," ed. Eleanor Damon Pace, *Southwestern Historical Quarterly*, 32 (1929), 298–99; C. K. Stribling to Col. Amasa Turner, *Batchelor-Turner Letters, 1861–1864*, annot. H. J. H. Rugeley (Austin, Texas: Steck Co., 1961), p. 88 (hereafter cited as BTL); Jesse C. Lane to Julia Turner Batchelor ("Friend"), BTL, pp. 81–2; William T. and Sallie Turner to "Brother and Sister," BTL, pp. 82–5; C. K. Holman to Frances I. Gilliam, "From Paraclifta to Marks' Mill: The Civil War Correspondence of Lieutenant

Robert C. Gilliam," ed. James J. Hudson, *Arkansas Historical Quarterly*, 17 (1958), 301-2; John C. Curtwright to Mr. and Mrs. L. B. Lovelace, *War Was the Place* (Chattahoochee Valley Historical Society, Bulletin 5, November, 1961), pp. 48, 51-2 (hereafter cited as *WWP*); J. W. Oslin to "Bro Dormon," *WWP*, p. 119; Nannie A. Pond to Jacob Miller, *WWP*, p. 115; Mrs. H. F. Wyche to Mrs. Miller, *WWP*, pp. 115-7; Ansel Sterne to "Friend," *WWP*, pp. 73-4; Thomas Jefferson Hodnett to "Father Mother Brothers and Sisters," *WWP*, pp. 76-7, 80-1; W. T. Hall to Marshall C. Newberry, "The Civil War Letters of Thomas Jefferson Newberry," ed. Enoch L. Mitchell, *Journal of Mississippi History*, 10 (1948), 80; W. J. O'Daniel to Sarah Torrence, "The Road to Gettysburg; the Diary and Letters of Leonidas Torrence of the Gaston Guards," ed., Haskell Monroe, *North Carolina Historical Review*, 36 (1959), 514-7; Kate V. Brand to Mrs. Boyd, "Casper W. Boyd, Company I., 15th Alabama Infantry, C. S. A., A Casualty of the Battle of Cross Keys, Virginia, His Last Letters Written Home," *Alabama Historical Quarterly*, 23 (1961), 297-8; C. Dicken to Mrs. Faney Catenhead [sic], "Some Confederate Letters of I. B. Cadenhead, Co. H., 34th Alabama Infantry Regiment, *Alabama Historical Quarterly*, 18 (1956), 567-8 (hereafter cited as *AHQ*); James T. Moore to Mrs. Cadenhead, *AHQ*, 568-9; I. G. Patten to Mrs. Cadenhed [sic], *AHQ*, 569; Levi Sowers to Emley Huckaby, "A Mississippian in Lee's Army: The Letters of Leander Huckaby," ed. Donald E. Reynolds, *Journal of Mississippi History*, 36 (1974), 287-8; W. H. D. Carrington to Mrs. Sallie Johnson, "Letters of John C. Johnson," ed. James M. Day, *Texana*, 4 (1966), 56-8 (hereafter cited as *Texana*); W. F. Robinson to Mrs. Johnson, *Texana*, 58-9; B. L. Goforth to Mrs. Sallie Johnson, *Texana*, 59-60; M. B. Locke to Dr. James David Rumph, "Letters of a Teenage Confederate," eds. Henry Eugene Sterkx and Brooks Thompson, *Florida Historical Quarterly*, 38 (1959-60), 343-6; Dr. A. E. McGarity to Rev. Edmund Cody, "Letters of Barnett Hardeman Cody and Others, Part II," contrib. Edmund Cody Burnett, *Georgia Historical Quarterly*, 23 (1939), 371-2 (hereafter cited as *GHQ*); W. C. Oats to Rev. Edmund Cody, *GHQ*, 372-3; Rev. Philip Slater Fall to "My Beloved Children," "Civil War Letters of Albert Boult Fall; Gunner for the Confederacy," *Register of the Kentucky Historical Society*, 59 (1961), 164-7; John S. Wise to Mrs. Ellen Bankhead Stanard, *Letters of a New Market Cadet*, eds. John G. Barrett and Robert K. Turner, Jr. (Chapel Hill, N. C.: University of North Carolina Press, 1961), pp. 67-8.

CHAPTER 6

1. This version of the model is in Beatrice B. Whiting and John W. M. Whiting, *Children of Six Cultures; A Psycho-Cultural Analysis* (Cambridge, Mass.: Harvard University Press, 1975), p. xvi. See also, for a discussion and critique of it, John W. M. Whiting, *A Model for Psycho-Cultural Research*, Distinguished Lecture, Annual Report 1973 (Washington: American Anthropological Association, 1974), pp. 1-14, and Erika Bourguignon, *Psychological Anthropology; An Introduction to Human Nature and Cultural Differences* (New York: Holt, Rinehart, and Winston, 1979), pp. 141-144.

2. Alvin Gouldner and Richard Peterson, *Notes on Technology and the Moral Order* (Indianapolis: Bobbs-Merrill, 1962).

3. Ibid., p. xii.

4. Ibid., p. 36.

5. Ibid., p. 39.

6. Ibid., p. 38. Their remark meshes well with Svend Ranulf's conclusion that "the disinterested tendency to inflict punishment is a distinctive characteristic of the lower middle class, that is, of a social class living under conditions which force its members to an extraordinary degree of self-restraint, and subject them to much frustration of natural desires." *Moral Indignation and Middle Class Psychology; A Sociological Study* (1938; rpt. New York: Schocken Paperback ed., 1964), p. 198.

7. Wesley C. Becker, "Consequences of Different Kinds of Parental Discipline," in Martin L. Hoffman and Lois Wladis Hoffman, eds., *Review of Child Development Research*, vol. I (New York: Russell Sage Foundation, 1964), p. 198.

8. Ibid., p. 191-193.

9. Ibid., pp. 195–197.

10. Ibid., p. 200.

11. Ibid., p. 177.

12. Ibid., p. 177.

13. Of course, child-rearing is not simply the discipline a child receives, but the consequences of discipline are more often studied by psychologists than other features of a child's existence. See also, Martin L. Hoffman, "Childrearing Practices and Moral Development: Generalizations from Empirical Research," *Child Development*, 34 (1963), 295–318.

14. See Jay Mechling, "Advice to Historians on Advice to Mothers," *Journal of Social History*, 9 (1975), 45–63.

15. See Philip Greven, ed., *Child-Rearing Concepts, 1628–1861; Historical Sources* (Itasca, Ill.: F. E. Peacock, 1973); Bernard Wishy, *The Child and the Republic; The Dawn of Modern American Child Nurture* (Philadelphia: University of Pennsylvania Press, 1972); Robert Sunley, "Early Nineteenth Century American Literature on Child Rearing," in Margaret Mead and Martha Wolfenstein, eds., *Childhood in Contemporary Cultures* (Chicago: University of Chicago Press, 1955); Daniel Calhoun, *The Intelligence of a People* (Princeton: Princeton University Press, 1973), pp. 134–205; and Nancy F. Cott, "Notes toward an Interpretation of Antebellum Childrearing," *Psychohistory Review*, vol. 6, no. 4 (Spring, 1978), 4–20, which is incorrectly numbered on its cover page as "vol. 7, no. 1."

16. See Karen Horney, *The Neurotic Personality of Our Time* (New York: W. W. Norton, 1937), and Erik Erikson, *Childhood and Society*, 2nd ed. (New York: W. W. Norton, 1963).

17. See Daniel Levinson, "The Changing Character of Middle Adulthood in American Society," in Gordon J. DiRenzo, ed., *We, The People; American Character and Social Change* (Westport, Conn.: Greenwood Press, 1977), pp. 147–177.

18. See Robert H. Bremner, *From the Depths; The Discovery of Poverty in the United States* (New York: New York University Press, 1956); John G. Cawelti, *Apostles of the Self-Made Man; Changing Concepts of Success in America* (Chicago: University of Chicago Press, 1965); and Irvin G. Wyllie, *The Self-Made Man in America; The Myth of Rags to Riches* (New York: Free Press, 1954).

19. Walter George Smith, *Life and Letters of Thomas Kilby Smith, Bvt. Major-General, U. S. Volunteers, 1820–1887* (New York: G. P. Putnam's Sons, 1898), pp. 345–346.

20. E. B. Tylor, the anthropologist, and Herbert Spencer, the popular intellectual, believed this. See Elvin Hatch, *Theories of Man and Culture* (New York: Columbia University Press, 1973), p. 51. See also, George M. Frederickson, *The Black Image in the White Mind; The Debate on Afro-American Character and Destiny, 1817–1914* (New York: Harper Torchbooks, 1972); William R. Stanton, *The Leopard's Spots: Scientific Attitudes Toward Race in America, 1815–1859* (Chicago: University of Chicago Press, 1960); Lawrence J. Friedman, *The White Savage: Racial Fantasies in the Postbellum South* (Englewood Cliffs, N. J.: Prentice-Hall, 1970); and Winthrop D. Jordan, *The White Man's Burden; Historical Origins of Racism in the United States* (London: Oxford University Press, 1974).

21. See Eric T. Carlson and Norman Dain, "The Meaning of Moral Insanity," *Bulletin of the History of Medicine*, 36 (1962), 130–140; Norman Dain and Eric T. Carlson, "Moral Insanity in the United States, 1835–1836," *American Journal of Psychiatry*, 118 (1962), 795–800; and Norman Dain, *Concepts of Insanity in the United States, 1789–1865* (New Brunswick, N. J.: Rutgers University Press, 1964).

22. See Charles Rosenberg, *The Trial of the Assassin Guiteau; Psychiatry and Law in the Gilded Age* (Chicago: University of Chicago Press, 1968).

23. See Eric T. Carlson and Norman Dain, "The Psychotherapy that was Moral Treatment," *American Journal of Psychiatry*, 116 (1960), 519–524.

24. See Barbara Welter, "The Cult of True Womanhood: 1820–1860," *American Quarterly*, 18 (1966), 151–174 and all the excellent essays by Charles Rosenberg and Carol Smith-Rosenberg, especially Charles Rosenberg, "Sexuality, Class, and Role in 19th Century America," *American Quarterly*, 25 (1973), 131–153.

25. The most revealing evidence has been collected and wisely discussed in a very useful book of readings. See Ronald G. Walters, ed., *Primers for Prudery; Sexual Advice to Victorian America* (Englewood Cliffs, N. J.: Prentice-Hall, 1974). Other useful studies are, G. J. Barker-Benfield, *The Horrors of the Half-Known Life; Male Attitudes Toward Women and Sexuality in Nineteenth-Century America* (New York: Harper Colophon ed., 1977); John S. Haller, Jr., and Robin M. Haller, *The Physician and Sexuality in Victorian America* (New York: W. W. Norton, 1977); and David J. Pivar, *Purity Crusade; Sexual Morality and Social Control, 1868–1900* (Westport, Conn.: Greenwood Press, 1974).

26. Benjamin Rush, *Medical Inquiries and Observations, Upon the Diseases of the Mind* (Philadelphia: Kimber and Richardson, 1812), pp. 351–356, quoted in Walters, *Primers*, pp. 111–112.

27. J. H. Kellogg, *Plain Facts about Sexual Life* (Battle Creek, Mich.: Office of the Health Reformer, 1877), pp. 249–260, quoted in Walters, *Primers*, pp. 37–39.

29. See Walters, *Primers*, p. 6.

29. Jules Henry, *Culture Against Man* (New York: Vintage Books, ed., 1965), p. 30.

30. William Alfred Hines, *American Communities* (New York: Office of the American Socialist, 1875), p. 164.

31. John Humphrey Noyes quoted in Walters, *Primers*, p. 132.

32. William Heartsill, *Fourteen Hundred and Ninety-One Days in the Confederate Army* (1876; rpt. Jackson, Tenn.: McCowat-Mercer Press, 1954), p. xiv.

33. Minne Clare Yarborough, ed., *The Reminiscences of William C. Preston*, in Willard Thorp, ed., *A Southern Reader* (New York: Alfred A. Knopf, 1955), p. 257.

34. Hugh C. Bailey, ed., "An Alabamian at Shiloh: The Diary of Liberty Independence Nixon," *Alabama Review*, 11 (1958), 147.

35. Harvey L. Carter and Norma L. Peterson, eds., "William S. Stewart Letters, January 13, 1861, to December 4, 1862," *Missouri Historical Review*, 61 (1967), 311.

36. Rev. William L. Lucey, ed., "The Diary of Joseph B. O'Hagan, S. J., Chaplain of the Excelsior Brigade," *Civil War History*, 6 (1960), 402–409.

37. John Perry Pritchett, "On the March with Sibley in 1863: The Diary of Private Henry J. Hagadorn," *North Dakota Historical Quarterly*, 5 (1930), 105–129.

38. Gertrude Himmelfarb, *Victorian Minds* (New York: Alfred A. Knopf, 1968), p. 276.

39. H. Barry, III, I. L. Child, and M. K. Bacon, "Relation of Child Training to Subsistence Economy," *American Anthropologist*, 61 (1959), 51–63.

40. Richard D. Brown, *Modernization; The Transformation of American Life, 1600–1865* (New York: Hill and Wang, 1976). See also Brown, "Modernization and the Modern Personality in Early America, 1600–1865: A Sketch of a Synthesis," *Journal of Interdisciplinary History*, 2 (1972), 201–228.

41. Philip Greven, *The Protestant Temperament; Patterns of Child-Rearing, Religious Experience, and the Self in Early America* (New York: Knopf, 1977).

42. Ibid., pp. 318–319.

43. J. G. Randall and David Donald, *The Civil War and Reconstruction*, 2nd ed. (Boston, D. C. Heath, 1961), p. 66.

44. Charles Grier Sellers, Jr., "The Travail of Slavery," in Sellers, ed., *The Southerner as American* (1960; rpt. New York: E. P. Dutton, 1966), p. 67n.

45. W. J. Cash, *The Mind of the South* (New York: Vintage, 1941), p. 51. A view somewhat different from Cash's was recorded in 1870 by a visitor to the South from Edinburgh, who found the black preachers "very rude and uncultivated" but concluded that the former slaves were "the only people I ever met whose religion reacted on their daily life." To be sure, the idea of religion applied to living may have struck a genteel Southerner as romantic if not downright hedonistic. See Leon F. Litwack, *Been in the Storm So Long: The Aftermath of Slavery* (New York: Knopf, 1979), p. 459, and Dickson D. Bruce, Jr., "Religion, Society, and Culture in the Old South: A Comparative View," *American Quarterly*, 26 (1974), 399–416.

46. Winthrop D. Jordan, *The White Man's Burden; Historical Origins of Racism in the United States* (London: Oxford University Press, 1974), p. 222.

47. Quoted in Thomas Bright, "Yankees in Arms: The Civil War as a Personal Experience," *Civil War History*, 19 (1973), 211.

48. Mildred Throne, ed., "A Commissary in the Union Army: Letters of C. C. Carpenter," *Iowa Journal of History*, 53 (1955), 87.

49. John E. Pomfret, ed., "Letters of Fred Lockley, Union Soldier, 1864–65," *Huntington Library Quarterly*, 16 (1952–53), 110.

50. Henry Adams, *The Education of Henry Adams*, Ernest Samuels, ed., (Boston: Houghton Mifflin Riverside edition, 1973).

51. "Letters of Major Thomas Rowland, C.S.A. from North Carolina, 1861 and 1862," *William and Mary College Quarterly Historical Magazine*, 25 (1916), 79.

52. William L. Wilson, *A Borderland Confederate*, Festus P. Summers, ed. (Pittsburgh: University of Pittsburgh Press, 1962), p. 27.

53. William F. Pendleton, *Confederate Diary: Capt. W. F. Pendleton, January to April, 1865* (Bryn Athyn, Pa.: Privately printed, 1957), p. 12. See also Steven M. Stowe, "The 'Touchiness' of the Gentleman Planter: The Sense of Esteem and Continuity in the Antebellum South," *Psychohistory Review*, 8 (Winter, 1979), 6–15. Stowe's essay was published after my research was completed. We did not know about one another's work, but we came to many of the same conclusions.

54. Victor Houghton, *The Victorian Frame of Mind* (New Haven: Yale University Press, 1957), pp. xiv–xv.

Appendix I

CHARACTERISTICS OF THE SAMPLE

The entire study was based on the published Civil War diaries and letters of 419 persons. That total includes 185 soldiers' diaries, 216 soldiers' letter collections (over 3600 letters), and 30 separate letters of condolence written usually by soldiers but sometimes by civilian men and women. (Those three numbers add up to 431, not 419, because 12 soldiers wrote more than one kind of document.)

The first phase of the study, the content analysis of core values in chapter 2, was based on the diaries of 100 soldiers—25 Northern officers, 25 enlisted Northerners, 25 Southern officers, and 25 enlisted Southerners. The second phase of the study, the content analysis of character values in chapter 3, was based on the same sample of 100 diarists. The third phase of the study, the key word counts in chapter 3, was based on 300 diaries and letter collections: the original 100 diaries and 200 letter collections by 50 Northern officers, 50 enlisted Northerners, 50 Southern officers, and 50 enlisted Southerners. The fourth phase of the study, the style counts in chapter 4, was based on approximately 360,000 words from 292 diaries and letter collections: 185 diaries (by 53 Northern officers, 62 enlisted Northerners, 35 Southern officers, and 35 enlisted Southerners), and 107 letter collections (by 32 Northern officers, 28 enlisted Northerners, 23 Southern officers, and 24 enlisted Southerners).

The original 100 diaries were used in all phases of the study—the core values analysis, character values analysis, key word counts, and style counts. The 85 additional diaries were used only in the style counts (for 28 Northern officers, 37 enlisted Northerners, 10 Southern officers, and 10 enlisted Southerners). Among the letter collections, 216 in all, 109 were counted only for key terms, 16 only for style, and 91 for both key terms and style.

The diaries and letters were selected from a master list of published personal documents compiled mainly from annual bibliographies in the *Journal of American History* and *Civil War History*; E. Merton Coulter's *Travels in the Confederate States*; Charles E. Dornbusch's *Military Bibliography of the Civil War*, volumes 1 and 2; and Allan Nevins, James I. Robertson, Jr., and Bell Wiley's *Civil War Books; A Critical Bibliography*, volumes 1 and 2. Diaries were not included in the master list if they were too brief, if they had had too much text left out by the editor, or if they were not authentic diaries, such as memoirs and field notes transcribed into diaries many years after the war. About three-fourths of the diaries in the original sample of 100 were complete, and the remainder were sufficient excerpts. Nearly all the letter collections contained three or more letters. The sources are not a random sample selected from a universe of available documents. Indeed, the sources are a kind of "universe" in themselves—they represent all the documents which were acceptable and could be obtained.

The sample is limited in several respects. It contains no blacks, almost no recent immigrants, few urbanites, few old men, and no women except in a special instance. Of all the men in the United States eligible for military service, it includes only those Civil War soldiers who kept diaries or wrote letters and whose diaries or letters survived to be published. There are probably about 2000 separately published Civil War diaries and letter collections available in this country. Many of these published personal documents, however, would not be suitable for a study such as this one; indeed, I had to reject about as many diaries as I accepted. This sample of 430 probably contains about one-fourth to one-third of all the suitable documents available. I have copies of all the documents that were used.

How are published diaries and letters different from unpublished ones? I put this question to archivists and also studied it myself. Before the 1960s it was ordinarily the case that the more "interesting" documents were published, of course. But during the Civil War Centennial a good many less interesting diaries and letters were published simply because they were topical. Also, it has lately been true that editors and owners of documents have strived to publish the ordinary documents of ordinary soldiers; most of the famous and best documents had been published earlier, in any case. It is probably true that the descendants of highly educated soldiers, who are apt to be highly educated themselves today, are more likely to submit their ancestors' documents for publication than the less educated descendants of less educated soldiers. Also, the less educated descendants are probably less likely to donate a personal document to an archive where a scholar might find it and prepare it for publication. In other words, there may be differences between published diaries and letters and unpublished ones still locked up in trunks. This sample, however, contains a fairly wide variety of documents, and our research has shown that an author's education appeared to have no significant effect on the characteristics of his diary or letter which we chose to study. Therefore, it seems reasonable to conclude that a similar study of unpublished documents would not necessarily have produced very different results from those obtained in this study with these documents. Those who doubt this claim are invited to study as many unpublished personal documents from the Civil War and present their evidence. Many of our findings, incidentally, agree with Bell Wiley's, and his studies have been based mainly on unpublished documents.

Despite its shortcomings, this sample has many strengths. It consists of spontaneous private documents written by an unusually large number of men who were living under roughly similar conditions at the same time. Many of them were probably unusual Americans—better educated than most, more observant than most, more likely to have had the "itch to record" and all that that implies—but perhaps as many in the sample were otherwise representative Americans. Moreover, simply because men were unusual in those respects does not mean that they are bad informants; in fact, they may be the best informants we can get for a study of culture and personality. Cultural anthropologists who have recorded the life histories of informants willing to give them have made this same kind of defense of their "biased" data. In short, this sample may come about as close to "laboratory conditions" as we can in such historical studies.

The Diarist Identification Form (Fig. 3) was completed for each of the original 100 diarists. All the results on the nineteen variables were then concatenated with one another by using the CROSSTABS computer program from the Statistical Package for the Social Sciences (SPSS). This program produced over 300 tables which made it possible to identify virtually any sub-group in the sample, such as Confederate volunteer infantry sergeants from the rural lower South who were under 30, unmarried, and with little education. Then the recorded value expressions of that sub-group could be identified and compared with those of any other sub-group in the sample of 100 diarists. The data which have been drawn from those tables are only a smidgen of the total available. They are the most significant smidgen, however.

What follows is a variable-by-variable description of the characteristics of the original sample of 100 diarists. Wherever possible the characteristics of the sample are compared with those of the armies or the population at large.

Unit Membership (C)

About three-quarters of the soldiers in the two armies were probably infantrymen. In our sample 76.5 percent are infantrymen. There are no Northern artillerymen in the sample, but otherwise the two distributions are similar: Northern infantry, 86.0 percent of the Northern sample; Southern infantry, 66.7 percent of the Southern sample; Northern cavalry, 12.0 percent of the Northern sample; Southern cavalry, 18.8 percent of the Southern sample.

Fig. 3   Diarist Identification Form

A. DIARIST NO.

B. ARMY MEMBERSHIP
   1 USA   2 CSA

C. UNIT MEMBERSHIP
     1 Cavalry   3 Infantry   5 Other _____
     2 Artillery   4 Mixed membership___ 6 Unknown

D. REGIONAL ORIGIN
     1 Northeast (ME,VT,NH,MA,CT,RI,NY,PA,NJ)
     2 Northwest (OH,MI,MN,IN,IL,IA,WI)
     3 Far West (CA,OR,Territories)
     4 Border States (DE,MD,WV,KY,MO)
     5 Upper South (VA,NC,TN,AR)
     6 Lower South (SC,GA,AL,MI,LA,TX)
     7 Mixed Origin _____
     8 Other _____
     9 Unknown

E. COMMUNAL ORIGIN
     1 Rural, small farm   4 Mixed origin_____
     2 Small town   5 Other _____
     3 City, urban   6 Unknown

F. YEAR OF BIRTH   (Last two digits; leave blank if unknown)

G. MARITAL EXPERIENCE
     1 Never married 2 Married currently or previously
     3 Unknown

H. EDUCATION (partial or completed)
     1 Primary (grades one thru eight)   4 No formal education
     2 Secondary, Academy   5 Other
     3 College, Law School, Medical school 6 Unknown

I. PREVIOUS OCCUPATION   (Describe _____)
     1 Professional and semi-professional   7 Service work
     2 Farmers and farm managers   8 Farm work
     3 Proprietors, managers, officials   9 Laborer
     4 Clerical, sales, and kindred   10 Mixed_____
     5 Craftsmen, and kindred   11 Other_____
     6 Operatives and kindred   12 Unknown

J. POST-WAR OCCUPATION (Describe _____)
     1 thru 12 (see codes above)   14 Retired
     13 Killed in war or died soon after 15 Moved West

K. PREDOMINATE RANK IN DIARY
     1 Private   6 Enlisted-staff
     2 Corporal, Sergeant   7 Officer-staff
     3 Lieutenant, Captain   8 Other_____
     4 Major, Lt. Col, Colonel 9 Unknown
     5 General

L. RANK PROGRESS
     1 Elected by subordinates or peers   4 Never promoted
     2 Appointed, promoted, commissioned 5 Mixed methods_____
       by superiors   6 Other _____
     3 Increase in rank, but method unknown 7 Unknown

M. ENTRY PROCESS
     1 Volunteer   3 Bounty Soldier   5 Other _____
     2 Draftee   4 Raised Unit   6 Unknown

N. RELIGIOUS AFFILIATION
     1 Baptist   5 Presbyterian   9 Protestant
     2 Roman Catholic 6 Episcopal   10 None
     3 Lutheran   7 Jewish   11 Other
     4 Methodist   8 Congregational 12 Unknown

Fig. 3   Diarist Identification Form (continued)

O.   LITERARY STYLE
       1 Verbose, articulate, cultured, graphic
       2 Plain, homespun, phonetic spelling, but graphic
       3 Primarily weather or march log
       4 Other _____

P.   ETHNIC ORIGIN   (Diarist's last name _____)
       DIARIST   MOTHER   FATHER   ANCESTORS
       1 American-born   4 Canadian-born   7 French-born
       2 German-born   5 English-born   8 Other_____
       3 Irish-born   6 Scandinavian-born 9 Unknown

Q.   FATHER'S/GUARDIAN'S OCCUPATION
       (Describe _____)
       1 thru 12 (use codes from category "I")

R.   POLITICAL PREFERENCE
       1 Republican   3 Other_____
       2 Democrat   4 Unknown

S.   ESTIMATED WEALTH-CLASS-STATUS BACKGROUND
       1 Upper   4 Other_____
       2 Middling   5 Unknown
       3 Lower

MISCELLANEOUS (Describe any other significant characteristics of
     the diarist or his background not included above.)

Regional Origin (D)

Regional origin refers to the region of the country in which the soldier was born or spent most of his life before the war. Troops from the Northeast (Maine, Vermont, New Hampshire, Massachusetts, Connecticut, Rhode Island, New York, Pennsylvania, and New Jersey) comprise 32 percent of the Northern sample; these same states actually made up about 47 percent of the nation's male population in 1860 (all national statistical data came from the 1960 edition of *Historical Statistics of the United States*). The Northwestern states (Ohio, Michigan, Minnesota, Indiana, Illinois, Iowa, and Wisconsin) contribute 60 percent of the soldiers in the Northern sample, but those states only constituted about 35 percent of the male population of the Northern states in 1860. This imbalance between the two regions in the Northern sample is probably due to the fact that Northwestern state historical societies, especially in Illinois and Indiana, have encouraged the publication of more of their citizens' diaries than have the other states.

Eight percent of the Southern soldiers in the sample were former residents of the North; that figure is probably high for the Southern army as a whole. No soldiers from the Border states (Delaware, Maryland, West Virginia, Kentucky, and Missouri) are included in the Northern sample. However, 20 percent of the soldiers in the Southern sample were from Border states, and 8 percent were from the Northeast or the Northwest; both these figures are probably high for the Southern army as a whole. Apparently the editors of journals have been more interested in the diaries of "defectors" to the South.

Soldiers from the Upper South (Virginia, North Carolina, Tennessee, and Arkansas) constitute 26 percent of the Southern sample, while those states made up about 53 percent of the white male population of the South in 1860. This discrepancy may be a result of the emphasis on "defectors" in the Southern sample and the practices of editors of journals. Soldiers from the lower South (South Carolina, Georgia, Alabama, Mississippi, Louisiana, and Texas, excluding Florida) constitute 42 percent of the Southern sample; those states actually contained about 47 percent of the Southern white male population in 1860.

Communal Origin (E)

Communal origin refers to the type of "local group" the soldier was born or spent most of his life in before the war. A total of 80.9 percent of the men in the Northern sample are classified as coming from rural (single farm) or town (less than 2500 population) settings; a total of 81.6 percent of the men in the Southern sample is also classified as rural or town. National census data reveal that 80.2 percent of the total population were living in rural or town settings in 1860; actual North-South figures are not available. Twenty cases in the sample, however, were coded as "unknown" on this matter, 12 of them from the South. I would suspect that most of these missing cases were born and raised on farms, which is the most likely characteristic of one's origin to be unrecorded or unknown to the editor of the diary.

Year of Birth (F)

Diarist's age refers to the age of the diarist in 1861. The sample is weighted in favor of 20-year-olds and against older men and adolescents, which is in accord with the composition of the armies (the average age of the Civil War soldier was about 26). The age categories for both armies are distributed as follows:

Ages of Diarists

Diarist's age in 1861	Percent of total sample	Percent of total males (age 15 to 60+) in nation in 1860
16 – 20	10.9	18 (age 15 – 19)
21 – 29	54.3	30 (age 20 – 29)
30 – 39	26.1	22
40 – 49	7.6	15
50 – 59	0.0	8
60+	1.1	7

Age distributions within the two armies are difficult to assess accurately. Bell Wiley has written that about 75 percent of the Union army were under 30 years of age in 1863; the comparable figure for our Northern sample is 72.4 percent. However, he also says that in the first year of the war the largest single age group in the Union army was 18-year-olds, and the next largest category was 20-year-olds; this sample is not quite that young. Wiley states that about one-half percent of the Union soldiers in his large sample were between 46 and 65 years of age; our sample shows that 6.4 percent of the Northern soldiers were over 40 years of age. This discrepancy is probably due to the greater number of older officers in our sample.

The Southern soldiers in the sample are slightly older than the norm for both North and South. Soldiers from age 16 to 29 are 57.8 percent of the Southerners in the sample; Wiley's sample showed that about 80 percent were under 30. Southern soldiers in their 30s are 31.3 percent of the Southern sample, while Wiley's Southern sample consisted of about 16 percent 30-year-olds. Southern soldiers over 40 years of age are 11.1 percent of the Southern sample, compared to 6.4 percent in the Northern sample and to about 5 percent in Wiley's Southern sample. There were 8 cases of missing data in the total sample. Perhaps older soldiers, especially among Confederates, were a bit more likely to keep diaries. Again, the fact that one-half of the Southern sample were officers has probably skewed the age distribution in favor of older men.

Marital Experience (G)

Marital status refers to whether the soldier was (1) never married before or during the course of his diary, or (2) currently married, widowed, or divorced during the course of his diary. Compared to the national data, the sample is weighted in favor of the unmarried. Of all the soldiers in the sample, 57.8 percent were thought to be unmarried; the national figure for 1890, the only available year close to the date of the war, is 33 percent. Surprisingly, Southerners in the sample differ from Northerners in the sample in this regard: 64.4 percent of the Union soldiers were unmarried, compared to 50.0 percent of the Southerners. Ten cases were classified as unknown. In some cases coders made estimates on this matter, depending on the types of mentions of women made in the diaries. It is possible that this cautious estimating caused the number of unmarried to be over-rated, since if there were no women mentioned in the diary, one might code the diarist unmarried, especially if he were young. It was probably not uncommon, as Wiley states, for young, rural volunteers—a large portion of the sample—to be bachelors in the 1860s, so the sample probably reflects that tendency. Many of the diarists married after the war.

Education (H)

Education refers to the soldier's level of education, in process or completed, in 1861. The distribution on this variable is the most unrepresentative of any in the sample. Even if all the missing cases (29) were classified as having just a little schooling, the sample would still be heavily weighted in favor of college students or graduates (this includes all students and graduates in legal studies and medical studies).

National data indicate that 59 percent of all white males between the ages of 5 and 19 were in some school in 1850; 62 percent of the male children in that category were in school in 1860. Our known sample shows that 32.4 percent of all the soldiers (Northern, 36.4 percent; Southern, 29.0 percent) had completed or were in primary or secondary school, including academies, in 1861, and that 93 percent had completed or were in primary schools, secondary schools, or colleges in 1861. We are no doubt low on primary and secondary graduates and students because of the number of missing cases in the sample, and because the preponderance of college students and graduates squeezes out the non-college students. A total of 60.6 percent of the known sample soldiers were college students or graduates before the war (Northern, 57.6 percent; Southern, 63.2 percent). National data for 1870 show that only 1.7 percent of all persons aged 18 to 21 were in college. The additional number of college graduates or ex-college students living in 1870 would not raise the figure of 1.7 percent appreciably.

There are two apparent explanations for this gross distortion in the sample. The most obvious answer has to do with the initial decision to make half the sample consist of officers. When we examine education according to rank, we find that of the 43 "college" soldiers, 26 were officers (including all officers in the ranks from Major through General). But that still leaves 17 enlisted men who were classified as "college." Nine of these were privates. We know it was not uncommon at this time for undergraduates to want to serve out their time humbly as common soldiers; we also have been told that, in the Confederate army, they might find it hard to be elected to a higher rank even if they aspired to it. That may partly explain their presence among the enlisted ranks, but we still have not explained their general predominance in the total sample. Therefore, it may be that college students and graduates are much more likely to write diaries than anyone else, and it is probably even more likely that such men would have had highly-educated descendants who would make their diaries available for publication.

Previous Occupation (I)

This refers to the soldier's general category of occupation in 1861. Again, because officers are half the sample, and because the sample is highly educated, the distribution of occupations is not an accurate representation of the national distribution of occupations. Professionals and semi-professionals (including physicians, attorneys, teachers, editors, and the like) constitute 33.8 percent of the total sample (Northern, 25.0 percent, Southern, 42.1 percent), while the national figure was probably between 3 and 5 percent. Farmers and farm workers are 12.2 percent of the total sample (Northern, 11.2 percent; Southern, 13.2 percent), while the national figure was probably around 50 percent of the male population. Proprietors, managers, officials, clerical, sales, and kindred make up 13.6 percent of the total sample (Northern, 2.8 percent; Southern 23.7 percent), while the national figure for persons in "commercial" occupations was around 5 percent in 1860. Craftsman and the like are 9.5 percent of the total sample (Northern, 19.4 percent, Southern, 0 percent), while the national figure for "mechanics" was around 25 percent. The sample was also difficult to classify because so many persons had a variety of temporary occupations before the war. In 26 cases there was no information on this matter, and if we assume that all of those were probably farmers or farm workers then about one-third of the sample would be farmers. Most of the active students in the sample were categorized as "other" (18.9 percent) on the coding forms. If we may assume that these persons would not be counted as employed in the census of 1860, that would increase even more the relative percentage of farmers in the sample. In any case, we know that professionals are over-represented in the sample, and that there are unexplained North-South differences in the distribution of certain occupations, such as minor white collar workers.

Post-War Occupation (J)

This refers to the soldier's general category of occupation after he left the service. We have here roughly the same maldistribution in favor of professionals (39.7) percent) as was true of the pre-war occupational variable. No deserters are believed to be represented, and the number of men in the sample who died during the war is probably too high (17.8 percent).

Generally, we had great difficulty classifying the many post-war occupations a single soldier often had, so no attempt was made to correlate any findings with this variable. There were 27 cases of missing data.

Predominate Rank in Diary (K)

This refers to the rank that was held for the longest time during the course of the soldier's diary. This distribution was purposely stratified (25 enlisted men and 25 officers for each army) in order that the major categories of soldiers could be adequately represented and compared in the sample. Besides the planned over-representation of officers, we also found that soldiers in noncombatant staff positions were unintentionally over-represented (about 25 percent of all the officers in the sample were in staff positions). This may have been a function of the high levels of education among the soldiers in the sample. However, there is no reason to believe that the inclusion of a disproportionately high number of staff officers will substantially affect our results. The number of men at each rank in the sample was roughly similar for both North and South. The two most frequently occuring ranks were privates (24.0 percent) and lieutenants/captains (28.0 percent). Higher ranking enlisted men (corporals and sergeants, 18.0 percent) and officers (majors, lieutenant colonels, colonels, and generals, 10.0 percent) are over-represented. There were no missing data.

Rank Progress (L)

This refers to the soldier's method of increasing in rank during the course of his diary. In general, those who increased in rank by any means are probably over-represented (only 21.1 percent of the 100 soldiers had no promotion). This may be due, again, to the high educational levels of most soldiers in the sample. The 24 cases of missing data probably were not promotions, since a promotion would more often than not have been mentioned by the diarist or the diary's editor. But even if that is true, the sample is still biased in favor of "successful" soldiers. The major North-South difference lies in men promoted by appointment: North, 63.4 percent; South, 42.9 percent. Fifteen men in all (North, 6; South, 9) were elected to higher ranks at least once.

Entry Process (M)

This variable refers to the soldier's method of entering the army. Like most soldiers, 83.7 percent of the men in the sample were volunteers. Those officers who raised units (12.0 percent) are probably over-represented, while draftees and bounty soldiers (those who took another draftee's place for a fee) may be under-represented (3.3 percent). The 8 unknown cases were probably volunteers. There were no significant North-South differences in the sample.

Religious Affiliation (N)

This refers to the soldier's denominational affiliation or preference. We had hoped to acquire adequate data on this matter, but many of the codings are mainly guesses based on the soldier's mention of which church services he attended. Fifty-two percent were identified as "unclassified Protestant," but 28 cases were not coded. We have no reason to believe that the data are exceptionally biased on the matter of religion, but in any case this variable was not used for any explanations. There were no North-South differences among those soldiers in the sample who were classified.

Literary Style (O)

This refers to the diarist's style of writing, and its determination was strictly a matter of judgment. The choices were "verbose," (verbose, articulate, cultured, graphic), "plain" (plain, homespun, phonetic spelling, but graphic), and "log" (primarily a terse weather or march log). The codings support the stereotypes that are usually attributed to antebellum Northerners and Southerners. Eighty percent of the Confederates in the sample were classified as verbose, compared to 40 percent of the Northerners; 38 percent of the Northerners were short-winded log-keepers, compared to only 10 percent of the Southerners. Most of the diarists (60 percent) were considered verbose.

Ethnic Origin (P)

This variable refers to the diarist's country of birth or his effective ethnic orientation. Many of the soldiers in the sample were considered to be native-born because there was no mention by the diarist or the diary's editor that the author was foreign-born. Whether this was justified or not, the sample is weighted in favor of native-born males (94.7 percent). In 1860 about 81 percent of the white male population was actually native-born. While the samples of the two armies do not differ on this variable, Wiley has written that probably three-quarters of the Union troops were native-born, while the proportion of native-born Confederates was noticeably higher. The sample is also no doubt skewed because we selected only diaries that were originally written in English. All of the surnames of the diarists were of Northern European origin (English, Scottish, Irish, German, Scandinavian, French).

Father's Occupation (Q)

This refers to the occupation of the diarist's father before the author entered the service. We had hoped to be able to acquire such information in order to gain a better perspective on the diarist's socioeconomic background. What information we do have is somewhat closer to national norms than the data on the diarist's pre-war occupation (45.7 percent of the fathers were farmers; only 20.0 percent were professionals), but this information was so scarce that it was of no use (65 cases are unknown).

Political Preference (R)

This refers to the diarist's political preference, as expressed by his party affiliation or his voting behavior in the army. As with the previous variable, there was little evidence (79 cases unknown), so no use was made of this variable. All identified Republicans (9) were in the Union army, while all identified Democrats (10) were in the Confederate army.

Estimated Wealth-Class-Status Background (S)

This variable, somewhat like Literary Style, was based on our summary impression. Estimating a man's position in a society is a very debatable exercise, especially when one does not have access to information on his income or those of his peers in his community. Nevertheless, we made our estimates, based primarily on our knowledge of the diarist's occupation, education, and rank in service. We were hesitant to identify a man as upper class or lower class unless there was good evidence in the diary's text or its introduction to justify such a choice. Thus, 75.0 percent of all our soldiers are classified as "middling" in social status (Wiley states that most soldiers were of that background). There were twice as many upper class Confederates (31.9 percent of the Southern sample) as upper class Unionists (14.3 percent of the Northern sample), which is not surprising. Only 2.1 percent of all the soldiers were classified as lower class; they are surely under-represented in the sample, but they were perhaps not as likely to write diaries in any case.

Rank Progress During Career

This last variable is not listed on the Diarist Identification Sheet, for it is one that was made up from the previous variables after they had been coded. This variable was designed to indicate a soldier's general level of achievement during his entire military career, and thus to identify those enlisted men who were thought motivated and competent enough to become officers. Of the 25 Northern enlisted men (so classified because that was their predominate rank while writing their diaries), 4 eventually became officers. Of the 25 Southern enlisted men, 7 became officers. Of the 25 Northern officers, 8 came from the enlisted ranks, and of the 25 Southern officers, 4 came from enlisted ranks. There were insufficient data on 9 of the 50 Southern soldiers; these men were probably always enlisted men or always officers; otherwise the diarist or the diary's editor would have been likely to have mentioned such an important change. Again, the sample is biased in favor of "successful" soldiers. Perhaps those were the kinds of men most apt to write diaries, or the kinds of men most likely to have had their diaries preserved and published. Even so, it can be argued that such "successful" soldiers may have displayed the dominate values of their group even more than the "unsuccessful" soldiers. They might offer exaggerations, not perversions, of values and valued personality traits.

Characteristics of the Letter-writers

A less ambitious analysis of the backgrounds of the 200 letter-writers was made because the analysis of the diarists had shown which variables were likely to have biased results. The overall level of education among the letter-writers was still very high, but not so high as it was among the diarists. Among the officers, it was just as high: 26 of the 50 officers writing diaries were college students or graduates, lawyers or training for the law, physicians or training for medicine; 51 of the 100 officers writing letters had comparable education. It is interesting that those two ratios are so close. Among the enlisted men writing diaries, 17 of 50 had high education, of the enlisted men writing letters, only 12 out of 100 had high education. So the letter-writers, particularly the enlisted men, are closer to the norms of the general population. The regional origin of the letter-writers is also closer to what it should be. Eight percent of the Southern diarists were born or raised in the Northeast, and 20 percent of the Southern diarists were born or raised in the Border states. Both these figures are too high. But among the letter-writers who were South-erners, only 1 percent came from the Northeast and only 5 percent came from the Border states. Among the Southern letter-writers, however, a disproportionate number came from the lower South—65 percent. In a perfect sample, that figure would be 47 percent. The upper South is under-represented among Southern letter-writers exactly the same way as it is among Southern diarists—both groups of men comprise 26 percent of their samples, but they should be about 53 percent.

Editors of published letters do not seem to give as much background on the writers as editors of diaries, so much of the information on the pre-war occupations of the letter-writers was missing. Among the Northern enlisted men farmers were most often identified, along with a few craftsmen (such as a tinsmith, builder, tailor, mason, and mechanic), a few clerks, a few teachers, and a few students. All but one of these men came from farms or small towns. There were no factory workers among the Northern enlisted men who wrote letters. Almost all the Southern enlisted letter-writers were independent farmers or farmers' sons before the war. There was only one craftsman listed, a cabinet-maker. None of the Southern enlisted men came from large cities; in fact, many of these men were identified only by the county where they grew up. At least 16 of the 100 Southern officers and enlisted men who wrote letters had been born on plantations or owned them.

About half of all the Northern and Southern officers who wrote letters were highly educated or they were professionals. The remainder tended to be farmers, merchants, or clerks. Seven officers out of 100 had graduated from West Point and were professional soldiers. Again, there were almost no urbanites among the officers.

Appendix II

METHOD OF CONTENT ANALYSIS

Over a period of nine years a total of 82 coders analyzed the personal documents of the 430 writers. The coding of the core values was done by 6 students and me. The coding of the character values was done by 17 other students and me. The key word counts and style counts were done by 58 other students and me.

The following three coding forms show how we collected our data. Both the Core Values Coding Form (Fig. 4) and the Character Values Coding Form (Fig. 5) required us to locate and transcribe the value statements. The Character Values Coding Form also required us to specify the Attributes of the person being evaluated so that a "Referent Profile" could be constructed. These referent data, however, were not analyzed in this study. The Style Coding Form (Fig. 6) needs no explanation beyond what is already provided in Chapter 4, except to say that the data in the last three columns—counts of verbs, adjectives, and "types" (the number of different words in a 100 word string)—were collected so that verb-adjective ratios and type-token ratios could be calculated. These findings, however, were not included in this study.

The three facsimiles of computer print-out sheets show how all the character evaluations were processed. First, all the words in a diarist's character evaluations were keypunched on IBM cards (Fig. 7, Sample Listing of Diarist's Character Statements). Then, all the words in the statements were alphabetized and the context of each word was set beside it (Fig. 8, Sample KWIC [Key Word in Context] of a Diarist's Character Statements). Finally, all the words used in all 100 diarists' character statements were alphabetized, counted, and located by the diary identification numbers (Fig. 9, Sample of Final Character Term Dictionary). For example, the word "beautiful" was used by 20 diarists in their character statements. Diarist #001 used it once, #009 used it six times, and so on. The final dictionary thus allowed us to see which character terms were used most often, then the KWIC listing could show us how they were used. The five key character terms—kind, noble, gallant, brave, and gentleman—were discovered by this process.

All three groups of coders were trained before they were allowed to code for this study. It was not possible to have several coders work over the same document until they agreed. I checked samples of each coder's work, however, and eliminated from the study those results which were obviously flawed. The core value analysis is likely to contain the most errors because subtle and complex judgments had to be made and codified. The possibility of coder error was lower in the character value analysis because character evaluations were more easily identified. The counts of key words are probably very reliable, and also the style counts, because these were clerical tasks to a large degree. In any case, it is fair to presume that any errors made by the 82 coders are spread randomly across the four groups of soldiers.

One may wonder whether the same results would have emerged from civilian rather than military documents. There is no reason to believe that the style counts would change, but the core and character values might fall in a different order and the key words might change. This is because civilian documents speak of different matters than military documents. How often, for example, might a man refer to his neighbor as

Fig. 4   Core Values Coding Form

Diarist No.

Value Codes:

1 Achievement, success, competition
2 Activity, work
3 Moral-judgmental orientation
4 Humanitarian mores
5 Efficiency, practicality
6 Progress, optimism
7 Materialism, passive gratification
8 Equality
9 Freedom, liberty

10 External conformity
11 Science, secular reason
12 Patriotism (specify
      national, sectional,
      state, local, unit, etc.)
13 Democracy
14 Individualism, self-reliance
15 Religious
16 Other value-laden premises
      or statements

Page Date	Code	Positive-Negative	Explicit-Implicit	Value Expression

Fig. 5   Character Values Coding Form

Diarist No.

Referent:

A (Focus)
  1 Self
  2 Specific person
  3 People
  4 Other_____
  5 Unknown

B (Race)
  1 White
  2 Negro
  3 Other____
  4 Unknown

C (Sex)
  1 Male
  2 Female
  3 Both
  4 Unknown

D (Function)
  1 Soldier
  2 Civilian
  3 Other____
  4 Unknown

E (Section)
  1 Northern
  2 Southern
  3 Other____
  4 Unknown

F (Negroes)
  1 Slave
  2 Free
  3 Other____
  4 Unknown

G (Soldiers)
  1 Private
  2 Corporal, Sergeant
  3 Lieutenant, Captain
  4 Major, Lt. Col., Col.
  5 General
  6 Other _____
  7 Unknown

H (Relationship)
  1 Mother
  2 Father
  3 Wife
  4 Lover
  5 Relative _____

  6 Friend
  7 Impersonal
  8 Other _____
  9 Unknown

Date Page	Referent Profile							Character Values Expressed
	A	B	C	D	E	F	G	H

Fig. 6 Style Coding Form

Civil War Letters and Diaries

Letter Colletion no. _____ Diary no. _____

Total no. of Letters _____ Total no. Diary entries _____

Start date _____ End date _____ Total no. Days _____

Coder _____
Author _____
Complete _____ Excerpt _____

sampl item no.	total no. words	no. sylls 100 words	no. sents 100 words	avg no. words per sent	no. incom sents	no. egos 100 words	no. solid 100 words	no. detac 100 words	no. negs 100 words	no. explo 100 words	no. verbs 100 words	no. adjs 100 words	no. types 100 words
_____	_____	_____	_____	_____	_____	_____	_____	_____	_____	_____	_____	_____	_____
_____	_____	_____	_____	_____	_____	_____	_____	_____	_____	_____	_____	_____	_____
_____	_____	_____	_____	_____	_____	_____	_____	_____	_____	_____	_____	_____	_____
_____	_____	_____	_____	_____	_____	_____	_____	_____	_____	_____	_____	_____	_____
_____	_____	_____	_____	_____	_____	_____	_____	_____	_____	_____	_____	_____	_____
_____	_____	_____	_____	_____	_____	_____	_____	_____	_____	_____	_____	_____	_____

no. keywords

kind _____
noble _____
gentleman _____
brave _____
gallant _____

Fig. 7   Sample Listing of Diarist's Character Statements

REFERENT PROFILE

```
01.009.11112 4 .012
02.099.11112 4 .012
03.099.11112 4 .012
01.099.31322 7.012
02.099.31322 7.012
01.101.21322 5.012
02.101.21322 5.012
03.101.21322 5.012
04.101.21322 5.012
05.101.21322 5.012
06.101.21322 5.012
07.101.2.322 5.012
01.108.31112 70.012
02.108.31112 70.012
03.108.31112 70.012
01.117.31222 6.012
02.117.31222 6.012
03.117.31222 6.012
04.117.31222 6.012
01.192.221221 6.012
```

I BELIEVE I AM RIGHT AND I BELIEVE THAT GOD SMILES ON THOSE WHO ACT ACCORDING TO THE HONEST DICTATES OF THE HEART, WHICH HE MADE AND GAVE

CITIZENS, MALE AND FEMALE, VISIT US AND FROM THEM WE RECEIVE MUCH CHEER, SPIRITUAL AND BODILY.

AH! I NEVER YET KNOWN HOW TO APPRECIATE THE TRUE LOVE OF FOND AND DEVOTED PARENTS, IT CRUSHES MY HEART TO THINK OF LEAVING THEM WITH NO CHILD TO COMFORT THEIR DECLINING YEARS, BUT THE STRENGTH AND INTELLECT WHICH GOD GAVE ME MUST BE PUT TO USE. NOT FOLDED IN A NAPKIN, AND I BELIEVE THAT I AM DOING RIGHT. IN OTHER TIMES I HOPE TO RETURN AND FIND MY HOME AND STATE FREE.

IN THIS BATTLE SOME OF THE BRAVEST OF THE BRAVE AND NOBLEST OF THE NOBLE LAID DOWN THEIR LIVES, WILLING SACRIFICES ON THE ALTER OF LIBERTY.

HOW MANY OF THE NOBLEST, BEST AND MOST BEAUTIFUL OF THE FEMALE SEX LIKE THIS GOOD CREATURE TO WHOM I HAVE JUST BEEN TALKING, GROW UP IN THE WILD VALLEYS OF THE COUNTRY UNKNOWN, UNHONORED AND UNSUNG?

HE IS THE MOST FAITHFUL SLAVE I EVER KNEW. I SHALL SEND HIM

Fig. 8 Sample KWIC of a Diarist's Character Statement

Keyword	Context	Code	Value	No.
ACCEPTED	ACCEPTED. /SUBSTITUTES. THEY ARE FRAUDS AND SHOULD NOT BE	02.010.31119	07.024	1
ACCOMPLISHED	ACCOMPLISHED GENTLEMAN, A FINE OFFICER/RANKS. HE WAS	01.007.21112	46.024	2
ACT	ACT OF WHICH WE MAY WELL BE PROUD TO OUR DYING DAY.	03.030.31112	97.024	3
AFFAIR	AFFAIR, OF WHICH THE REGIMENT AND COUNTRY HAD CAUSE TO	03.020.21112	57.024	4
ALABAMIANS	ALABAMIANS CONFIDENT OF OUR ULTIMATE SUCCESS/HE REPORTS	01.004.31322	7.024	5
ARE	ARE A GREAT MEANS OF DIVERSION TO SOLDIERS. /THEATRES	00.003.9 9	9.024	6
2	ARE FRAUDS AND SHOULD NOT BE ACCEPTED. /SUBSTITUTES. THEY	02.010.31119	07.024	7
ARMY	ARMY OF NORTHERN /BATTLE'S BRIGADE IS THE FIRST IN	01.030.31112	97.024	8
AS	AS .ED, MAHONE OF AUBURN, BROUGHT ON FOUR IRISHMEN	01.010.31119	07.024	9
AT	AT HOME, SWEET HOME, WITH THE DEAREST OF /HAPPY DAYS	01.015.11112	39.024	10
AUBURN	AUBURN, BROUGHT ON FOUR IRISHMEN AS /ED. MAHONE, OF	01.010.31119	07.024	11
BATTLE'S	BATTLE'S BRIGADE IS THE FIRST IN THE ARMY OF NORTHERN	02.010.31119	07.024	13
2	BE PROUD TO OUR DYING DAY. /ACT OF WHICH HE MAY WELL	03.030.31112	97.024	14
BEASTLY	BEASTLY AND STEALTHY OF THE INHUMANE.	02.021.9 9	7.024	15
BELONG	BELONG TO SUCH A PATRIOTIC BODY OF HEROES./I REJOICE	00.030.11112	39.024	16
BEST	BEST OF SISTERS. /MOTHERS AND	02.015.11111	39.024	17
BODY	BODY OF HEROES./I REJOICE THAT I BELONG TO SUCH A	00.030.11112	39.024	18
BRAVE	BRAVE / I INTEND TO DO WHAT I MAY TO RELIEVE AND CHEER	02.006.31112	17.024	19

Fig. 9 Sample of Final Character Term Dictionary

BEAUREGARD'S	1	009	*	BECOME	1	034	*	BEEN	1	040	*	BEFORE	1	069		
BEAUTIES	1	054	*	BECOME	1	035	*	BEEN	5	047	*	BEFORE	3	070		
BEAUTIES	1	067	*	BECOME	1	061	*	BEEN	1	043	*	BEFORE	1	071		
BEAUTIFUL	1	001	*	BECOME	1	092	*	BEEN	3	045	*	BEFORE	2	078		
BEAUTIFUL	1	005	*	BECOME	1	093	*	BEEN	6	046	*	BEFORE	1	083		
BEAUTIFUL	1	006	*	BECOME	1	094	*	BEEN	1	047	*	BEFORE	1	085		
BEAUTIFUL	6	009	*	BECOME	1	100	*	BEEN	2	049	*	BEFORE	1	094		
BEAUTIFUL	1	012	*	BECOMES	1	034	*	BEEN	1	050	*	BEFORE	1	095		
BEAUTIFUL	2	016	*	BECOMES	1	066	*	BEEN	6	051	*	BEFORE	1	097		
BEAUTIFUL	1	023	*	BECOMING	1	009	*	BEEN	1	058	*	BEFORE	2	098		
BEAUTIFUL	3	027	*	BECOMING	1	028	*	BEEN	4	059	*	BEG	1	066		
BEAUTIFUL	1	032	*	BECOMING	1	062	*	BEEN	1	060	*	BEG	1	079		
BEAUTIFUL	5	034	*	BECOMING	1	098	*	BEEN	4	061	*	BEG	1	097		
BEAUTIFUL	3	037	*	BED	2	017	*	BEEN	4	062	*	BEGAN	1	005		
BEAUTIFUL	1	041	*	BED	1	024	*	BEEN	3	064	*	BEGAN	1	006		
BEAUTIFUL	1	045	*	BED	2	031	*	BEEN	2	066	*	BEGAN	1	007		
BEAUTIFUL	2	046	*	BED	1	033	*	BEEN	2	067	*	BEGAN	1	001		

"noble" and his grocer as "gallant"? One should not argue, however, that civilian documents thus offer "truer" data because they are written in normal times. They simply offer different data. Indeed, military service probably evokes more values and evaluations than civilian life, and combat probably puts a man "under a microscope" more often than peaceful conditions. I agree with what one of the soldiers wrote: "The minutia of character is here developed—which is ordinarily kept from the world." Military service was also likely to make diarists and letter-writers out of men who would have otherwise left no historical records if they had remained civilians, so our sample is wider and larger because we have used soldiers' personal documents.

The doctoral dissertation on which part of this study was based ("The Character of Civil War Soldiers: A Comparative Analysis of the Language of Moral Evaluation in Diaries," University of Pennsylvania, Department of American Civilization, 1974) has about 300 pages describing more completely the theory and method of content analysis, the theory and practice of core and character values, and the theory of personal documents. The dissertation relied only on the diaries of 100 soldiers; it does not include the data from the additional diaries and letters or the stylistic analysis.

Appendix III

TERMS OF THE CHARACTER MODEL

The following lists illustrate the terms exemplifying two value categories in the character model. If a soldier used the term "honest" in any of its grammatical forms, he was counted as having used the Moral character value once (see Fig. 10). If he used that term again or any other terms in that category, he still only received a count of "1" in that category for the group comparisons. All these terms were taken from remarks about character which coders identified in the original 100 diaries.

This procedure rests on the assumption that the use of the term signifies belief in the value. This assumption perhaps ought not to be made in the content analysis of very complex or vague values likely to be implicit in a remark. Thus, in the core value analysis the coders did not pin their judgments on the use of any particular terms. But in the content analysis of character values our experience convinced us that it was unusual for a soldier to write about anyone else's character or his own without using a specific character term. When a soldier, however, described himself or someone else in a way that was compatible with one of the character values, he was given credit for using that value even if he did not write down a specific character term. For example, if a man said his troops "must be put to use," he was given credit for Duty. I sorted the character terms

Fig. 10   Moral Terms

(+)	(−)
decent	wicked
virtuous	desperadoes
wise	depravity
Christian	profane
moral	corrupt
good	lewd
honest	debasing
upright	unholy
temperate	wretches
innocent	drunk
righteous	swearing
God	thieves
wholesome	cheat
pure	steal
	scoundrel

Fig. 11   Kind Terms

(+)	(−)
fond	mean
obliging	ruthless
charitable	greedy
humane	harsh
beloved	selfish
benefactor	beastly
generous	savage
liberal	barbarous
kind	ruffians
humble	cruel
nice	inhuman
affectionate	heartless
merciful	brute
lenient	relentless
indulgent	
love	

into the categories after examining every context of their use (of course, "fair weather" was not counted under Honorable, only a "fair man"). A man was also counted as using a category if he wrote down a negative term implying he believed in its opposite; for example, a soldier who remarked that a man was a "brute" received credit for using the character value Kind (see Fig. 11).

Sources

DIARIES

Northern Officers

Barnes, John Sanford. "The Battle of Port Royal. From the Journal of John Sanford Barnes, October 8 to November 9, 1861," Ed. John D. Hayes. *New-York Historical Society Quarterly*, 45 (1961), 365–95.

Bell, John N. "Diary of Captain John N. Bell of Co. E, 25th Iowa Infantry, at Vicksburg." *Iowa Journal of History*, 59 (1961), 181–221.

Brinton, Daniel Garrison. "From Chancellorsville to Gettysburg, A Doctor's Diary." Ed. D. G. Brinton Thompson. *Pennsylvania Magazine of History and Biography*, 89 (1965), 292–315.

Campbell, John Q. A. "The Civil War Diary of Lt. John Q. A. Campbell, Co. B, 5th Iowa Infantry." Ed. Edwin C. Bearss. *Annals of Iowa*, 3rd Ser., 39 (1967), 519–33.

Chapin, James W. "A Yank in the Carolina Campaign: The Diary of James W. Chapin, Eighth Indiana Cavalry." Ed. Donald E. Reynolds and Max H. Kele. *North Carolina Historical Review*, 46 (1969), 42–57.

Chase, Charles Monroe. "A Union Band Director Views Camp Rolla: 1861." Ed. Donald H. Welsh. *Missouri Historical Review*, 55 (1961), 307–43.

Churchill, Lee. "Extracts from the Diary of Captain Lee Churchill, One Hundred and Twenty-fifth Regiment, New York Volunteers." In *Fifth Annual Report of the Chief of the Bureau of Military Statistics, with Appendices*. Albany: C. Van Benthuysen and Sons Steam Printing House, 1868, pp. 559–68.

Clark, Leander. "Extracts from the Journal of Captain Leander Clark, Co. I, One Hundred and Twenty-fourth Regiment." In *Fifth Annual Report of the Chief of the Bureau of Military Statistics, with Appendices*. Albany: C. Van Benthuysen and Sons Steam Printing House, 1868, pp. 568–75.

Cogshall, Israel. "Journal of Israel Cogshall, 1862–1863." Ed. Cecil K. Byrd. *Indiana Magazine of History*, 42 (1946), 69–87.

Connolly, James A. *Three Years in the Army of the Cumberland: The Letters and Diary of Major James A. Connolly*. Ed. Paul M. Angle. Bloomington: Indiana University Press, 1959.

Dimon, Theodore. "A Federal Surgeon at Sharpsburg." Ed. James I. Robertson, Jr. *Civil War History*, 6 (1960), 134–51.

Dubois, John Van Deusen. "The Civil War Journal and Letters of Colonel John Van Deusen DuBois, April 12, 1961, to October 16, 1862." Ed. Jared C. Lobdell. *Missouri Historical Review*, 60 (1966), 436–59; 61 (1967), 21–50.

Ely Ralph. *With the Wandering Regiment: The Diary of Captain Ralph Ely of the Eighth Michigan Infantry.* Ed. George M. Blackburn. Mt. Pleasant, Michigan: Central Michigan University Press, 1965.

Gillet, Orville. "Diary of Lieutenant Orville Gillet, U. S. A., 1864–1865." Ed. Ted R. Worley. *Arkansas Historical Quarterly,* 17 (1958), 164–204.
Glover, Amos. "Diary of Amos Glover." Ed. Harry J. Carmen. *Ohio Historical Quarterly,* 44 (1935), 258–272.

Hamilton, Edward John. "A Union Chaplain's Diary." Ed. Chase C. Mooney. *Proceedings of the New Jersey Historical Society,* 75 (1957), 1–17.
Haviland, Thomas P. "A Brief Diary of Imprisonment." Contrib. Thomas P. Haviland. *Virginia Magazine of History and Biography,* 50 (1942), 230–37.
Higginson, Thomas Wentworth. "Camp Diary." In *Army Life in a Black Regiment.* 1869; rpt. Boston: Beacon Press, 1962, pp. 6–61.
Holmes, Oliver Wendell, Jr. *Touched With Fire: Civil War Letters and Diary of Oliver Wendell Holmes, Jr., 1861–1864.* Ed. Mark De Wolfe Howe. Cambridge: Harvard University Press, 1946.
Horton, Dexter. "Diary of an Officer in Sherman's Army Marching Through the Carolinas." Ed. Clement Eaton. *Journal of Southern History,* 9 (1943), 238–54.
Hughes, Frank. "Diary of Lieutenant Frank Hughes." Ed. Norman Niccum. *Indiana Magazine of History,* 45 (1949), 275–284.

Irwin, Samuel S. "Excerpts from the Diary of Samuel S. Irwin, July 5, 1863 to July 17, 1863." James Monahan. *Journal of Mississippi History,* 27 (1965), 390–94.

Jackson, Samuel McCartney. *Diary of General S. M. Jackson for the Year 1862.* Apollo, Pa.: privately printed, 1925.

Klock, Jacob C. "Letters to Friends [and diary extracts] from Major Jacob C. Klock, One Hundred and Fifty-third Regiment, New York Volunteers." In *Fifth Annual Report of the Chief of the Bureau of Military Statistics, with Appendices.* Albany: C. Van Benthuysen and Sons Steam Printing House, 1868, pp. 661–77.

Lennon, Martin. "Letters and Extracts from Diary of Captain Martin Lennon, of Company I, Seventy-seventh Regiment of New York State Volunteers." In *Fifth Annual Report of the Chief of the Bureau of Military Statistics, with Appendices.* Albany: C. Van Benthuysen and Sons Steam Printing House, 1868, pp. 714–56.

Mackey, James F. "Diary of Maj. James F. Mackey." In *History of the 103d Pennsylvania Volunteer Infantry, 1861–65.* Luther S. Dickey. Chicago: L. S. Dickey, 1910, pp. 314–40.
Mann, Nehemiah Halleck. "Extracts from Diary of Captain Nehemiah Halleck Mann, Company M, Fourth New York State Volunteer Cavalry." In *Fifth Annual Report of the Chief of the Bureau of Military Statistics, with Appendices.* Albany: C. Van Benthuysen and Sons Steam Printing House, 1868, pp. 617–31.
Mayfield, Leroy S. "A Hoosier Invades the Confederacy: Letters and Diaries of Leroy S. Mayfield." Ed. John D. Barnhart. *Indiana Magazine of History,* 39 (1943), 144–91.
McCoy, James. "Extracts from the Journal of Captain James McCoy, Twenty-second Regiment, New York State Volunteers." In *Fifth Annual Report of the Chief of the Bureau of Military Statistics, with Appendices.* Albany: C. Van Benthuysen and Sons Steam Printing House, 1868, pp. 544–59.
McIntyre, Benjamin F. *Federals on the Frontier: The Diary of Benjamin F. McIntyre, 1862–1864.* Ed. Nannie M. Tilley. Austin: Universitiy of Texas Press, 1960.

Morgan, John S. "Diary of John S. Morgan, Company G, Thirty-third Iowa Infantry." *Annals of Iowa*, 3rd Ser., 13 (1923), 483–508, 570–610.

Mosman, Chesley A. "Mosman's Diary. The Following is from a Diary Kept by C. A. Mosman, Late Lieutenant Company D, Fifty-ninth Illinois Infantry. . . ." In *Episodes of the Civil War*. George Washington Herr. San Francisco: Bancroft Co., 1890, pp. 361–97.

O'Hagan, Joseph B. "The Diary of Joseph B. O'Hagan, S. J., Chaplain of the Excelsior Brigade." Ed. Rev. William L. Lucey. *Civil War History*, 6 (1960), 402–9.

Parmelee, Uriah Nelson. *The Civil War Diary of Captain Uriah Nelson Parmelee, A Son of Guilford*. Ed. Charles Lewis Biggs. Guilford, Conn.: privately printed, 1940.

Patrick, Marsena Rudolph. *Inside Lincoln's Army: The Diary of Marsena Rudolph Patrick, Provost Marshal General, Army of the Potomac*. Ed. David S. Sparks. New York: Thomas Yoseloff, c1964.

Patten, James Comfort. "An Indiana Doctor Marches with Sherman: The Diary of James Comfort Patten." Ed. Robert G. Athearn. *Indiana Magazine of History*, 49 (1953), 405–22.

Pearson, Benjamin Franklin. "Benjamin Franklin Pearson's War Diary." *Annals of Iowa*, 3rd Ser., 15 (1925), 83–129.

Phillips, John Wilson. "The Civil War Diary of John Wilson Phillips." Ed. Robert G. Athearn. *Virginia Magazine of History and Biography*, 62 (1954), 95–123.

Raynor, William H. "The Civil War Experiences of an Ohio Officer at Vicksburg: Diary of Colonel William H. Raynor, 56th Ohio Infantry." Ed. Edwin C. Bearss. *Louisiana Studies*, 9 (1970), 246–300.

Rogall, Albert. "The Civil War Diary of Colonel Albert Rogall." Frank Levstik. *Polish American Studies*, 27 (Spring-Autumn, 1970), 33–79.

Root, William H. "The Experience of a Federal Soldier in Louisiana in 1863." Intro. by Walter Prichard. *Louisiana Historical Quarterly*, 19 (1936), 635–67.

Sedgwick, Arthur G. "Libby Prison: The Civil War Diary of Arthur G. Sedgwick." By William M. Armstrong. *Virginia Magazine of History and Biography*, 71 (1963), 449–60.

Small, Abner R. *The Road to Richmond: The Civil War Memoirs of Maj. Abner R. Small of the 16th Maine Volunteers, with his Diary as a Prisoner of War*. Ed. Harold Adams Small. Berkeley: University of California Press, 1957.

Smith, John Henry. "The Civil War Diary of Colonel John Henry Smith." Ed. David M. Smith. *Iowa Journal of History*, 47 (1949), 140–70.

Snowden, George Randolph. "Home to Franklin! Excerpts from the Civil War Diary of George Randolph Snowden." Charles H. Ness. *Western Pennsylvania Historical Magazine*, 54 (1971), 158–66.

Strother, David Hunter. *A Virginia Yankee in the Civil War: The Diaries of David Hunter Strother*. Ed. Cecil D. Eby, Jr. Chapel Hill: University of North Carolina Press, c1961.

Taylor, Robert B. "The Battle of Perryville, October 8, 1862, as Described in the Diary of Captain Robert B. Taylor," Ed. Hambleton Tapp. *Register of the Kentucky Historical Society*, 60 (1962), 255–92.

Tourgée, Albion W. "A Civil War Diary of Albion W. Tourgée." Ed. Dean H. Keller. *Ohio History*, 74 (1965), 99–131.

Tracy, Albert. "Fremont's Pursuit of Jackson in the Shenandoah Valley: The Journal of Colonel Albert Tracy, March–July 1862." Ed. Francis F. Wayland. *Virginia Magazine of History and Biography*, 70 (1962), 165–93, 332–54.

Turner, William H. "Diary of W. H. Turner, M. D., 1863." Ed. Mildred Throne. *Iowa Journal of History*, 48 (1950), 267–82.

Wainwright, Charles S. *A Diary of Battle: The Personal Journals of Colonel Charles S. Wainwright, 1861–1865*. Ed. Allan Nevins. New York: Harcourt, Brace, and World, c1962.

Warmoth, Henry Clay. "The Vicksburg Diary of Henry Clay Warmoth: Part I (April 3, 1863–April 27, 1863)." Ed. Paul H. Hass. *Journal of Mississippi History*, 31 (1969), 334–47; "The Vicksburg Diary of Henry Clay Warmoth: Part II (April 28, 1863–May 26, 1863)." Ed. Paul H. Hass. *Journal of Mississippi History*, 32 (1970), 60–74.

Weld, Stephen Minot. *War Diary and Letters of Stephen Minot Weld, 1861–1876.*. Cambridge, Mass.: Riverside Press, 1912.

Southern Officers

Alison, Joseph Dill. "War Diary of Dr. Joseph Dill Alison of Carlowville, Alabama." *Alabama Historical Quarterly*, 9 (1947), 385–98.

Bedford, A. M. "Diary Kept by Capt. A. M. Bedford, Third Missouri Cavalry, while on Morris Island, S. C., Prisoner of War at Hilton Head and Fort Pulaski." In *The Immortal Six Hundred*. John O. Murray. n.p., 1911, pp. 250–319.

Brown, John Henry. "'The Paths of Glory' (The War-time Diary of Maj. John Henry Brown, C.S.A.)." Ed. W. J. Lemke. *Arkansas Historical Quarterly*, 15 (1956), 344–59.

Cox, Abner R. "South From Appomatox: The Diary of Abner R. Cox." Ed. Royce Gordon Shingleton. *South Carolina Historical Magazine*, 75 (1974), 238–44.

Craig, J. M. "The Diary of Surgeon Craig, Fourth Louisiana Regiment, C.S.A., 1864–65." John S. Kendall. *Louisiana Historical Quarterly*, 8 (1925), 53–70.

Fleming Robert H. "The Confederate Naval Cadets and the Confederate Treasure: The Diary of Midshipman Robert H. Fleming." Ed. G. Melvin Herndon. *Georgia Historical Quarterly*, 50 (1966), 207–16.

Fullam, George Townley. *The Journal of George Townley Fullam, Boarding Officer of the Confederate Sea Raider Alabama*. Ed. Charles G. Summersell. University, Ala.: University of Alabama Press, 1973.

Gailor, Frank M. "The Diary of a Confederate Quartermaster." Eds. Charlotte Cleveland and Robert Daniel. *Tennessee Historical Quarterly*, 11 (1952), 78–85.

Garnett, James Mercer. "Diary of Captain James M. Garnett, Ordnance Officer of Rodes's Division, 2d Corps, Army of Northern Virginia, From August 5th to November 30th, 1864, covering part of General Early's Campaign in the Shenandoah Valley." *Southern Historical Society Papers*, 27 (1899), 1–16; 28 (1900), 58–71.

Gorgas, Josiah. *The Civil War Diary of General Josiah Gorgas*. Ed. Frank E. Vandiver. University, Ala.: University of Alabama Press, 1947.

Gray, Richard L. "Prison Diary of Lieutenant Richard L. Gray." In *Diaries, Letters, and Recollections of the War Between the States*. Winchester-Frederick County Historical Society Papers, Winchester, Virginia. Vol. 3, 1955, pp. 30–45.

Hall, James E. *The Diary of a Confederate Soldier, James E. Hall*. Ed. Ruth Woods Dayton. Charleston, W. Va.: privately printed, 1961..

Harris, John H. "Diary of Captain John H. Harris." In *Confederate Stamps, Old Letters, and History*. Raynor Hubbel. Privately printed, 1959, pp. 2–13.

Key, Thomas J. *Two Soldiers: The Campaign Diaries of Thomas J. Key, C.S.A., December 7, 1863–May 17, 1865, and Robert J. Campbell, U.S.A., January 1, 1864–July 21, 1864*. Ed. Wirt Armistead Cate. Chapel Hill: University of North Carolina Press, 1938.

Killgore, Gabriel M. "Vicksburg Diary: The Journal of Gabriel M. Killgore." Ed. Douglas Maynard. *Civil War History*, 10 (1964), 33–53.

McCreary, James Bennett. "The Journal of My Soldier Life." Contribs. Robert N. McCreary and Mrs. Gatewood Gay. *Register of the Kentucky Historical Society*, 33 (1935), 97–117, 191–211.

McGavock, Randal W. *Pen and Sword: The Life and Journals of Randal W. McGavock, Colonel, C.S.A.* Ed. Jack Allen. Nashville: Tenn. Historical Commission, 1959.

Mechling, William T. "William T. Mechling's Journal of the Red River Campaign, April 7–May 10, 1864." Ed. Alwyn Barr. *Texana*, 1 (1963), 363–79.

O'Brien, George W. "The Diary of Captain George W. O'Brien, 1863." Ed. Cooper W. Ragan. *Southwestern Historical Quarterly*, 67 (1963), 26–54, 235–46, 413–33.

Page, Richard C. M. "Diary of Major R. C. M. Page, Chief of Confederate States Artillery, Department of Southwest Virginia and East Tennessee, from October, 1864, to May, 1865." *Southern Historical Society Papers*, 16 (1888), 58–68.

Park, Robert Emory. "War Diary of Capt. Robert Emory Park, Twelfth Alabama Regiment, January 28th, 1863–January 27th, 1864. Accounts of the Battles of Chancellorsville, Gettysburg, Jeffersonton, Bristow Station, Locust Grove, Mine Run, the March into Maryland and Pennsylvania, with Reminiscences of the Battle of Seven Pines." *Southern Historical Society Papers*, 26 (1898), 1–31.

Pendleton, William Frederic. *Confederate Diary: Capt. W. F. Pendleton, January to April, 1865.* Bryn Athyn, Pa.: privately printed, 1957.

Semmes, Raphael. "Admiral on Horseback: The Diary of Brigadier General Raphael Semmes, February–May, 1865." Ed. W. Stanley Hoole. *Alabama Review*, 28 (1975), 129–50.

Shaffner, J. F., Sr. *Diary of Dr. J. F. Shaffner, Sr., commencing September 13, 1863, ending February 5, 1865.* [Ed. C. L. Shaffner.] Privately printed [c1936].

Sheeran, James B. *Confederate Chaplain: A War Journal of Rev. James B. Sheeran, 14th Louisiana, C.S.A.* Ed. Rev. Joseph T. Durkin. Milwaukee: Bruce Publishing Co., 1960.

Smith, Isaac Noyes. "A Virginian's Dilemma (The Civil War diary of Isaac Noyes Smith in which he describes the activities of the 22nd Regiment of Virginia Volunteers, Sept. to Nov., 1861)." Ed. William C. Childers. *West Virginia History*, 27 (1966), 173–200.

Steele, Nimrod Hunter. "The Nimrod Hunter Steele Diary and Letters." In *Diaries, Letters, and Recollections of the War Between the States.* Winchester-Frederick County Historical Society Papers, Winchester, Va. Vol. 3, 1955, pp. 48–57.

Stevenson, William Grafton. "Diary of William Grafton Stevenson, Captain, C.S.A." Ed. Carl Rush Stevenson. *Alabama Historical Quarterly*, 23 (1961), 45–72.

Taylor, Thomas J. "'An Extraordinary Perseverance,' The Journal of Capt. Thomas J. Taylor, C.S.A." Eds. Lillian Taylor Wall and Robert M. McBride. *Tennessee Historical Quarterly*, 31 (1972), 328–59.

Trimble, Isaac Ridgeway. "The Civil War Diary of General Isaac Ridgeway Trimble." Ed. William Starr Myers. *Maryland Historical Magazine*, 17 (1922), 1–20.

Vaughan, Turner. "Diary of Turner Vaughan, Co. 'C.' 4th Alabama Regiment, C.S.A., Commenced March 4th, 1863 and Ending February 12th, 1864." *Alabama Historical Quarterly*, 18 (1956), 573–604.

Wescoat, Joseph Julius. "Diary of Captain Joseph Julius Wescoat, 1863–1865." Ed. Anne King Gregorie. *South Carolina Historical Magazine*, 59 (1958), 11–23, 84–95.

Womack, James J. *The Civil War Diary of Capt. J. J. Womack, Co. E, Sixteenth Regiment, Tennessee Volunteers, (Confederate).* McMinnville, Tenn.: Womack Printing Co., 1961.

Woolwine, Rufus James. "The Civil War Diary of Rufus J. Woolwine." Ed. Louis H.
    Manarin. *Virginia Magazine of History and Biography*, 71 (1963), 416–48.
Wright, Marcus Joseph. "Diary of Brigadier-General Marcus Joseph Wright, C.S.A.,
    from April 23, 1861, to February 26, 1863." *William and Mary College
    Quarterly*, 2nd Ser., 15 (1935), 89–95.

Northern Enlisted

Affeld, Charles E. "Pvt. Charles E. Affeld Describes the Mechanicsburg Expeditions."
    Ed. Edwin C. Bearss. *Illinois State Historical Society Journal*, 56 (1963),
    233–56; "Pvt. Charles E. Affeld Reports Action West of the Mississippi." Ed.
    Edwin C. Bearss. *Illinois State Historical Society Journal*, 60 (1967), 267–96.
Alley, Charles. "Excerpts from the Civil War Diary of Lieutenant Charles Alley,
    Company 'C,' Fifth Iowa Cavalry." Ed. John S. Ezell. *Iowa Journal of History*,
    49 (1951), 241–56.
Ames, Amos. "A Diary of Prison Life in Southern Prisons." *Annals of Iowa*, 3rd Ser.,
    40 (1969–71), 1–19.

Bancroft, Albert H. "Diary of Albert H. Bancroft, Corporal of Co. B., Eighty-fifth
    Regiment, N.Y.S.V."In *Fifth Annual Report of the Chief of the Bureau of
    Military Statistics, with Appendices*. Albany: C. Van Benthuysen and Sons
    Steam Printing House, 1868, pp. 575–612.
Bensell, Royal Augustus. *All Quiet on the Yamhill, the Civil War in Oregon: The
    Journal of Corporal Royal A. Bensell, Company D, Fourth California
    Infantry*. Ed. Gunter Barth. Eugene: University of Oregon Books, 1959.
Benson, William C. "Civil War Diary of William C. Benson." *Indiana Magazine of
    History*, 23 (1927), 333–64.
Bigelow, Edwin B. "Edwin B. Bigelow, A Michigan Sergeant in the Civil War." Ed.
    Frank L. Klement. *Michigan History*, 38 (1954), 193–252.
Biggert, Florence C. "Some Leaves From a Civil War Diary." Ed. Harry R. Beck.
    Western Pennsylvania Historical Magazine, 42 (1959), 363–82.
Brady, John J. "Journal of John J. Brady, Color Corporal, Twelfth Regiment N.Y.S.V."
    In *Fifth Annual Report of the Chief of the Bureau of Military Statistics, with
    Appendices*. Albany: C. Van Benthuysen and Sons Steam Printing House,
    1868, pp. 438–73.
Brinkerhoff, Arch M. "Diary of Private Arch M. Brinkerhoff, Co. H, 4th Iowa Infantry,
    at Vicksburg." Ed. Edwin C. Bearss. *Iowa Journal of History*, 59 (1961),
    225–37.

Campbell, Robert J. *Two Soldiers: The Campaign Diaries of Thomas J. Key, C.S.A.,
    December 7, 1863–May 17, 1865, and Robert J. Campbell, U.S.A., January 1,
    1864–July 21, 1864*. Ed. Wirt Armistead Cate. Chapel Hill: University of North
    Carolina Press, 1938.
Clarke, John T. "The Diary of a Civil War Soldier with Sherman in Georgia."
    Bulletin of the Missouri Historical Society, 8 (1952), 356–70.
Cleveland, Edmund J. "The Second Battle of Cold Harbor, as Seen Through the Eyes
    of a New Jersey Soldier (Private Edmund J. Cleveland, Co. K, Ninth New
    Jersey Volunteers, 1st Brigade, 2nd Division, 18th Corps); June 1 to June 14,
    1864." Ed. Edmund J. Cleveland, Jr. *Proceedings of the New Jersey Historical
    Society* 66 (1948), 25–37; "The Siege of Petersburg . . . June 14–September 19,
    1804 [sic]," 66 (1948), 76–96; "The Siege of Petersburg . . . July 30–September
    19, 1804 [sic]," 66 (1948), 176–96; "The Campaign of Promise and Disappoint-
    ment . . . March 17–May 27, 1864," 67 (1949) 218–40, 308–28.
Colton, Matthias Baldwin. *The Civil War Journal and Correspondence of Matthias
    Baldwin Colton*. Ed. Jessie Sellers Colton. Philadelphia: Macrae-Smith Co.,
    1931.

Cox, Jabez Thomas. "Civil War Diary of Jabez Thomas Cox." *Indiana Magazine of History*, 28 (1932), 40–54.
Crary, Jerry. *Jerry Crary, 1842-1936: Teacher, Soldier, Industrialist.* Warren, Pa.: Newell Press, 1960.

Dougherty, William Thompson. "Civil War Diary of an Ohio Volunteer." Ed. Donald J. Coan. *Western Pennsylvania Historical Magazine*, 50 (1967), 171–86.
Doyle, James M. "The Diary of James M. Doyle." *Mid-America*, 20 (1938), 273–83.

Eberhart, James W. "Diary of Salisbury Prison by James W. Eberhart, Sergt. Co. 'G' 8th Pa. Res. Vol. Cor(ps) Also Co. 'G' 191st Pa. Vet. Volunteer." Ed. Florence C. McLaughlin. *Western Pennsylvania Historical Magazine*, 56 (1973), 211–51.

Ferguson, Leonard C. "The Civil War Diaries of Leonard C. Ferguson." Notes by William A. Hunter. *Pennsylvania History*, 14 (1947), 196–224, 289–313.
Fletcher, Stephen Keyes. "The Civil War Journal of Stephen Keyes Fletcher." Contrib. Maxwell Keyes Fletcher, III; Ed. Perry McCandless. *Indiana Magazine of History*, 54 (1958), 141–90.
Fletcher, William B. "The Civil War Journal of William B. Fletcher." Ed. Loriman S. Brigham, *Indiana Magazine of History*, 57 (1961), 41–76.

Gardner, Henry R. "A Yankee in Louisiana: Selections from the Diary and Correspondence of Henry R. Gardner, 1862-1866." Eds. Kenneth E. Shewmaker and Andrew K. Prinz. *Louisiana History*, 5 (1964), 271–95..
Gulick, William O. "The Journal and Letters of Corporal William O. Gulick." Ed. Max H. Guyer. *Iowa Journal of History*, 28 (1930), 194–267, 390–455, 543–603.

Hagadorn, Henry J. "On the March with Sibley in 1863: The Diary of Private Henry J. Hagadorn." John Perry Pritchett. *North Dakota Historical Quarterly*, 5 (1930), 105–29.
Hegeman, George. "The Diary of a Union Soldier in Confederate Prisons." Ed. James J. Heslin. *New-York Historical Society Quarterly*, 41 (1957), 233–78.
Helmon, Howard. "A Young Soldier in the Army of the Potomac: Diary of Howard Helmon, 1862." Ed. Arthur W. Thurner. *Pennsylvania Magazine of History and Biography*, 87 (1963), 139–55.
Hull, Lewis Byram. "Soldiering on the High Plains: the Diary of Lewis Byram Hull, 1864-1866." Ed. Myra E. Hull. *Kansas Historical Quarterly*, 7 (1938), 3–53.

Ibbetson, William H. H. "[Diary, October 8, 1862, to August 8, 1864] William H. H. Ibbetson, Co. D, 122d Reg. Ill." *Publications of the Illinois State Historical Library*, no. 37, 1930, pp. 236–73

James, Frederic Augustus. *Frederic Augustus James's Civil War Diary: Sumter to Andersonville.* Ed. Jefferson J. Hammer. Rutherford, N. J.: Fairleigh Dickinson University Press, 1973).

Kitts, John Howard. "The Civil War Diary of John Howard Kitts." *Transactions of the Kansas Historical Society*, 14 (1918), 318–32.
Koempel, Phil. *Phil Koempel's Diary, 1861-1865.* Privately printed, n.d..

Letteer, Alfred, W. "Andersonville. Diary of a Prisoner. From the Original Manuscript, Now First Printed." *Historical Magazine*, 2nd Ser., 9 (1871), 1–7.

Mackley, John. "The Civil War Diary of John Mackley." Ed. Mildred Throne. *Iowa Journal of History*, 48 (1950), 141–68.
Macy, William Madison. "The Civil War Diary of William M. Macy." *Indiana Magazine of History*, 30 (1934), 181–97.

Matthews, James Louis. "Civil War Diary of Sergeant James Louis Matthews." Ed.
Roger C. Hackett. *Indiana Magazine of History*, 24 (1928), 306–16.
McKinley, William. "A Civil War Diary of William McKinley." Ed. H. Wayne Morgan.
Ohio Historical Quarterly, 69 (1960), 272–90.
Mockett, Richard H. "The Richard H. Mockett Diary." Ed. James L. Sellers. *Mississippi
Valley Historical Review*, 26 (1939), 233–40.
Morse, Bliss. *Civil War Diaries of Bliss Morse*. Ed. Loren J. Morse. Pittsburgh, Kan.:
Pittcraft, 1964.

Nichols, Norman K. "The Reluctant Warrior: The Diary of N. K. Nichols." T. Harry
Williams. *Civil War History*, 3 (1957), 17–39.

Onderdonk, James H. "A Civil War Diary," Dino Fabris. *New York History*, 49
(1968), 76–89.

Pattison, John J. "With the U. S. Army Along the Oregon Trail, 1863–66; Diary by
Jno. J. Pattison." *Nebraska History Magazine*, 15 (1934), 79–93.
Paxson, Lewis C. "Diary Kept by Lewis C. Paxson, Stockton, N. J. (1862–64)."
Collections of the State Historical Society of North Dakota, 2 (1906), 102–63.

Rathbun, Isaac R. "A Civil War Diary: The Diary of Isaac R. Rathbun, Co. D,
86th N. Y. Volunteers, Aug. 23, 1862–Jan. 30, 1863." Ed. Lawrence R.
Cavanaugh. *New York History*, 36 (1955), 336–45.
Ray, George B. "Journal of George B. Ray, Musician, Co. 'H.' 5th Ohio Vol. Infantry;
Enlisted April 19th 1861—Discharged April 3d 1863." *Historical and Philo-
sophical Society of Ohio Publications*, (1926), 57–73.
Richards, David Allen. "The Civil War Diary of David Allen Richards." Ed. Frederick D.
Williams. *Michigan History*, 39 (1955), 183–220.
Robertson, Melville Cox. "Journal of Melville Cox Robertson." *Indiana Magazine of
History*, 28 (1932), 116–37.
Ross, Charles. "Diary of Charles Ross, 1862." *Vermont History*, 30 (1962), 85–148.

Sanders, Richard A. "The Civil War Diary of Richard Sanders." *Now and Then*,
12 (1961), 36–43, 151–62.
Seiser, August F. "August Seiser's Civil War Diary." Charles E. Seiser. *Rochester
Historical Society Publications*, 22 (1944), 174–98.
Sheldon, Charles LeRoy. "The Diary of a Drummer." Ed. John L. Melton. *Michigan
History*, 43 (1959), 315–48.
Smith, Benjamin T. *Private Smith's Journal; Recollections of the Late War*. Ed. Clyde C.
Walton. Chicago: Lakeside Press, R. R. Donnelley and Sons, 1963.
Starr, Darius. "From Spotsylvania Courthouse to Andersonville: A Diary of Darius
Starr." Ed. E. Merton Coulter. *Georgia Historical Quarterly*, 41 (1957), 176–90.
Stoddard, George N. "The 100th Regiment on Folly Island; from the Diary of Private
George N. Stoddard." *Niagara Frontier*, 1 (1954), 77–81, 113–16.

Taylor, Isaac Lyman. "Campaigning with the First Minnesota: A Civil War Diary."
Ed. Hazel C. Wolf. *Minnesota History*, 25 (1944), 11–39, 117–52, 224–57,
342–61.

Ward, Lester Frank. *Young Ward's Diary. A human and eager record of the years
between 1860 and 1870 as they were lived in the vicinity of the little town of
Towanda, Pennsylvania; in the field as a rank and file soldier in the Union
Army; and later in the nation's Capital, by Lester Ward, who became the first
great sociologist this country produced*. Ed. Bernhard J. Stern. New York:
G. P. Putnam's Sons, 1935.
White, Thomas Benton. "Down the Rivers: Civil War Diary of Thomas Benton White."
Ed. Charles G. Williams. *Register of the Kentucky Historical Society*, 67
(1969), 134–74.

Wilcox, Charles E. "Hunting for Cotton in Dixie: From the Civil War Diary of Captain Charles E. Wilcox." Ed. Edgar L. Erickson. *Journal of Southern History*, 4 (1938), 493–513; "With Grant at Vicksburg: From the Civil War Diary of Captain Charles E. Wilcox." Ed. Edgar L. Erickson. *Journal of the Illinois Historical Society*, 30 (1938), 440–503.

Wiley, Harvey W. "Corporal Harvey W. Wiley's Civil War Diary." William L. Fox. *Indiana Magazine of History*, 51 (1955), 139–62.

Willoughby, Charles H. "Extracts from Journal of Charles H. Willoughby, Private, Company C., Thirty-fourth New York Volunteers." In *Fifth Annual Report of the Chief of the Bureau of Military Statistics, with Appendices*. Albany: C. Van Benthuysen and Sons Steam Printing House, 1868, pp. 473–543.

Wilson, John. "An Illinois Soldier in North Mississippi: Diary of John Wilson, February 15–December 30, 1862." Ed. J. V. Frederick. *Journal of Mississippi History*, 1 (1939), 182–94.

Wright, John P. "Diary of Private John P. Wright, U. S. A., 1864–1865." Ed. Ralph R. Rea. *Arkansas Historical Quarterly*, 16 (1957), 304–18.

Southern Enlisted

Andrews, W. H. *Diary of W. H. Andrews, 1st Sergt. Co. M, 1st Georgia Regulars, from Feb. 1861, to May 2, 1865.* East Atlanta: n.p., 1891?

[Anonymous.] *A Confederate Diary of the Retreat From Petersburg, April 3–20, 1865.* Ed. Richard B. Harwell. Atlanta: The Library, Emory University, 1953.

Barrow, Willie Micajah. "The Civil War Diary of Willie Micajah Barrow, September 23, 1861–July 13, 1862." Eds. Wendell H. Stephenson and Edwin A. Davis. *Louisiana Historical Quarterly*, 17 (1934), 436–51, 712–31.

Chambers, William Pitt. "My Journal, 1862." *Publications of the Mississippi Historical Society*, NS, 5 (1925), 221–386.

Clement, Abram Wilson. "Diary of Abram W. Clement, 1865." Ed. Slann L. C. Simmons. *South Carolina Historical Magazine*, 59 (1958), 78–83.

Dodd, Ephraim Shelby. *Diary of Ephraim Shelby Dodd, Member of Company D, Terry's Texas Rangers, December 4, 1862–January 1, 1864.* Austin, Texas: Press of E. L. Stack, 1914.

Dodd, James M. "Civil War Diary of James M. Dodd of the 'Cooper Guards.'" *Register of the Kentucky Historical Society*, 59 (1961), 343–9.

Fauntleroy, James Henry. "Elkhorn to Vicksburg. [James H. Fauntleroy's Diary for the Year 1862]" Homer L. Calkin. *Civil War History*, 2 (1956), 7–43.

Hamilton, James Allen. "The Civil War Diary of James Allen Hamilton, 1861–1864." Ed. Alwyn Barr. *Texana*, 2 (1964), 132–45.

Hander, Christian Wilhelm. "Excerpts From the Hander Diary." Ed. and Trans. Leonard B. Plummer. *Journal of Mississippi History*, 26 (1964), 141–9.

Haney, John H. "Bragg's Kentucky Campaign: A Confederate Soldier's Account." Eds. Will Frank Steely and Orville W. Taylor. *Register of the Kentucky Historical Society*, 57 (1959), 49–55.

Haynes, Draughton Stith. *The Field Diary of a Confederate Soldier, Draughton Stith Haynes, While Serving With the Army of Northern Virginia, C.S.A.* Darien, Ga.: Ashantilly Press, 1963.

Heartsill, William Williston. *Fourteen Hundred and Ninety-One Days in the Confederate Army.* 1876; rpt. Jackson, Tenn.: McCowat-Mercer Press, 1954, pp. 269–92.

Hudson, James G. "A Story of Company D, 4th Alabama Infantry Regiment, C.S.A." Ed. Alma H. Pate. *Alabama Historical Quarterly*, 23 (1961), 139–79.

Kean, Robert Garlick Hill. *Inside the Confederate Government: The Diary of Robert Garlick Hill Kean.* Ed. Edward Younger. New York: Oxford University Press, 1957, pp. 3–27.

Leon, Louis. *Diary of a Tar Heel Confederate Soldier.* Charlotte, North Carolina: Stone Publishing Co., 1913.

Malone, Bartlett Yancey. *Whipt 'em Everytime: The Diary of Bartlett Yancey Malone, Co. H 6th N. C. Regiment.* Ed. William Whatley Pierson, Jr. Jackson, Tenn.: McCowat-Mercer Press, 1960.
Medford, Harvey C. "The Diary of H. C. Medford, Confederate Soldier, 1864." Eds. Rebecca W. Smith and Marion Mullins. *Southwestern Historical Quarterly,* 34 (1930), 106–40, 203–30.
Merz, Louis. "Diary of Private Louis Merz, C.S.A., of West Point Guards, 1862." *Bulletin of the Chatahoochee Valley Historical Society,* No. 4, 1959.
Moore, Robert Augustus. *A Life for the Confederacy, as Recorded in the Pocket Diaries of Pvt. Robert A. Moore, Co. G, 17th Mississippi Regiment Confederate Guards, Holly Springs, Mississippi,* Ed. James W. Silver. Jackson, Tenn.: McCowat-Mercer Press, 1959.
Morgan, George P. "A Confederate Journal." Ed. George E. Moore. *West Virginia History,* 22 (1961), 201–6.
Morgan, Stephen A. "A Confederate Journal." Ed. George E. Moore. *West Virginia History,* 22 (1961), 207–16.

Nixon, Liberty Independence. "An Alabamian at Shiloh: The Diary of Liberty Independence Nixon." Ed. Hugh C. Bailey. *Alabama Review,* 11 (1958), 144–55.

Patrick, Robert Draughton. *Reluctant Rebel: The Secret Diary of Robert Patrick, 1861–1865.* Ed. F. Jay Taylor. Baton Rouge: Louisiana State University Press, 1959.
Patterson, Edmund DeWitt. *Yankee Rebel: The Civil War Journal of Edmund DeWitt Patterson.* Ed. John G. Barnett. Chapel Hill: University of North Carolina Press, 1966.
Porter, William Clendenin. "War Diary of W. C. Porter." Ed. J. V. Frederick. *Arkansas Historical Quarterly,* 11 (1952), 286–314.

Seaton, Benjamin M. *The Bugle Softly Blows: The Confederate Diary of Benjamin M. Seaton.* Ed. Col. Harold B. Simpson. Waco: Texian Press, 1965.
Smith, James West. "A Confederate Soldier's Diary: Vicksburg in 1863." *Southwest Review,* 28 (1943), 293–327.
Smith, Thomas Crutcher. *Here's Yer Mule: The Diary of Thomas C. Smith, 3rd Sergeant, Company 'G,' Wood's Regiment, 32nd Texas Cavalry, C.S.A., March 30, 1862–December 31, 1862.* Waco: Little Texian Press, 1958.

Thompson, Joseph Dimmitt. "The Evacuation of Corinth, From the Diary and a Letter of Joseph Dimmitt Thompson." Ed. John G. Biel. *Journal of Mississippi History,* 24 (1962), 40–56.
Torrence, Leonidas. "The Road to Gettysburg: The Diary and Letters of Leonidas Torrence of the Gaston Guards." Ed. Haskell Monroe. *North Carolina Historical Review,* 36 (1959), 476–517.
Townsend, Harry C. "Townsend's Diary—January–May, 1965. From Petersburg to Appomattox, Thence to North Carolina to Join Johnston's Army." *Southern Historical Society Papers,* 34 (1906), 99–127.

West, John C. *A Texan in Search of a Fight. Being the Diary and Letters of a Private Soldier in Hood's Texas Brigade.* Waco, Texas: Press of J. S. Hill and Co., 1901; rpt. Waco, Texas: Texian Press, 1969.
Williamson, John Coffee. "The Civil War Diary of John Coffee Williamson." Ed. J. C. Williamson. *Tennessee Historical Quarterly,* 15 (1956), 61–74.

Wilson, William L. *A Borderland Confederate.* Ed. Festus P. Summers. Pittsburgh: University of Pittsburgh Press, 1962.

LETTERS

Northern Officers

Ames, William. "Civil War Letters of William Ames, From Brown University to Bull Run." Ed. William Greene Roelker. *Rhode Island Historical Society Collections*, 33 (1940), 73–92; 34 (1941), 5–24.

Baldridge, Samuel Coulter. "A Chaplain in the 11th Missouri Infantry." Ed. Wayne C. Temple. *Lincoln Herald*, 64 (1962), 81–88.
Beck, E. W. H. "Letters of a Civil War Surgeon." *Indiana Magazine of History*, 27 (1931), 132–63.
Bliss, Jesse C. "Letters From a Veteran of Pea Ridge." Eds. Paul R. Cooper and Ted R. Worley. *Arkansas Historical Quarterly*, 6 (1947), 462–71.
Bowditch, Charles P. "War Letters of Charles P. Bowditch." *Massachusetts Historical Society Proceedings*, 57 (1923–24), 414–95.
Braden, Robert F. "Selected Letters of Robert F. Braden, 1861–1863." Ed. Mrs. William R. Braden. *Indiana History Bulletin*, 41 (1964), 110–21.
Breck, George. "George Breck's Civil War Letters from the 'Reynold's Battery'." *Rochester Historical Society Publications*, 21 (1944), 91–149.

Capron, Thaddeus Hurlbut. "War Diary [and letters] of Thaddeus H. Capron, 1861–65." *Journal of the Illinois Historical Society*, 12 (1919), 330–406.
Carpenter, Cyrus Clay. "A Commissary in the Union Army: Letters of C. C. Carpenter." Ed. Mildred Throne. *Iowa Journal of History*, 53 (1955), 59–88.
Chamberlain, Valentine B. "A Letter of Captain V. Chamberlain, 7th Connecticut Volunteers." *Florida Historical Quarterly*, 15 (1936–37), 85–95.
Clark, George W. "Civil War Letters of George W. Clark." Ed. Gerald O. Haffner. *Register of the Kentucky Historical Society*, 62 (1964), 307–17.
Cox, Charles Harding. "The Civil War Letters of Charles Harding Cox." Contrib. Mrs. Caroline Cox Wyatt. Ed. Lorna Lutes Sylvester. *Indiana Magazine of History*, 68 (1972), 24–78, 181–239.
Curtis, Samuel Ryan. "'The Irrepressible Conflict of 1861'; The Letters of Samuel Ryan Curtis." Ed. Kenneth E. Colton. *Annals of Iowa*, 3rd Ser. 24 (1934), 14–58; "With Fremont in Missouri in 1861; The Letters of Samuel Ryan Curtis." Ed. Kenneth E. Colton. *Annals of Iowa*, 3rd Ser. 24 (1934), 104–67; "Frontier War Problems; Letters of Samuel Ryan Curtis." Ed. Kenneth E. Colton. *Annals of Iowa*, 3rd Ser. 24 (1934), 298–315.

Davis, Charles Lukens. "A Signal Officer with Grant: The Letters of Captain Charles L. Davis." Ed. Wayne C. Temple. *Civil War History*, (1961), 428–37.
Duncan, Charles Davenport. "The Correspondence of a Yankee Prisoner in Charleston, 1865." Contrib. John E. Duncan. *South Carolina Historical Magazine*, 75 (1974), 215–24.
Duren, Charles M. "The Occupation of Jacksonville, February 1864, and the Battle of Olustee. Letters of Lt. C. M. Duren, 54th Massachusetts Regiment, U. S. A." *Florida Historical Quarterly*, 32 (1953–54), 262–87.

Frank, Elijah H. "E. H. Frank to Catherine Varner, Charlotte, Iowa, 1862–63." *North Dakota Historical Quarterly*, 4 (1929–30), 186–96.

Garfield, James A. "Three Civil War Letters of James A. Garfield." Eds. James D. Norris and James K. Martin. *Ohio History*, 74 (1965), 247–52.

Grant, Ulysses S. *The Papers of Ulysses S. Grant*. Vol. 4. Ed. John Y. Simon. Carbondale, Ill.: Southern Illinois University Press, 1972.

Gray, John Chipman. *War Letters, 1862–1865, of John Chipman Gray, Major, Judge Advocate, and John Codman Ropes, Historian of the War*. Boston: Houghton Mifflin, 1927.

Greenleaf, Charles Henry. "The Greenleaf Civil War Letters." *Connecticut Historical Society Bulletin*, 26 (1961), 88–93.

Hadley, John V. "An Indiana Soldier in Love and War: The Civil War Letters of John V. Hadley." Ed. James I. Robertson, Jr. *Indiana Magazine of History*, 59 (1963), 189–288.

Harrison, Benjamin. *Benjamin Harrison 1833–1901, Chronology, Documents, Bibliographical Aids*. Ed. Harry J. Sievers. Dobbs Ferry, N. Y.: Oceana Publications, 1969.

Himoe, Stephen O. "An Army Surgeon's Letters to his Wife." Luther M. Kuhns. *Proceedings of the Mississippi Valley Historical Association*, 7 (1914), 306–20.

Hopkins, Owen Johnston. *Under the Flag of the Nation; Diaries and Letters of a Yankee Volunteer in the Civil War*. Ed. Otto F. Bond. Columbus, Ohio: Ohio State University Press, 1961.

Hough, Alfred Lacey. *Soldier in the West; The Civil War Letters of Alfred Lacey Hough*. Ed. Robert G. Athearn. Philadelphia: University of Pennsylvania Press, 1957.

Jordan, William H. "The Sixteenth Indiana Regiment in the Last Vicksburg Campaign." Ed. Willie D. Halsell. *Indiana Magazine of History*, 43 (1947), 67–82.

Kearney, Philip J. "Letters from the Field, Written to his Relatives, by Maj. Philip J. Kearney, Eleventh New Jersey Volunteers." *Historical Magazine*, 2nd Ser., 7 (1870), 184–95.

Klock, Jacob C. "Letters to Friends from Major Jacob C. Klock, One Hundred and Fifty-third Regiment, New York Volunteers." In *Fifth Annual Report of the Chief of the Bureau of Military Statistics, with Appendices*. Albany: C. Van Benthuysen and Sons Steam Printing House, 1868, pp. 661–77.

Lazear, Bazel F. "The Civil War Letters of Colonel Bazel F. Lazear." Ed. Vivian Kirkpatrick McLarty. *Missouri Historical Review*, 44 (1949–50), 254–73, 387–401; 45 (1950–51), 47–63.

Lennon, Martin [Michael?]. "Letters and Extracts from Diary of Captain Martin Lennon, of Company I, Seventy-seventh Regiment, New York State Volunteers." In *Fifth Annual Report of the Chief of the Bureau of Military Statistics, with Appendices*. Albany: C. Van Benthuysen and Sons Steam Printing House, 1868, pp. 714–756.

Lind, John Young. "The Civil War Letters of John Young Lind." Ed. Willard E. Wight. *Journal of the Presbyterian Historical Society*, 39 (1961), 76–87.

Lockley, Frederick E. "Letters of Fred Lockley, Union Soldier 1864–65." Ed. John E. Pomfret. *Huntington Library Quarterly*, 16 (1952–53), 75–112.

Lusk, William Thompson. *War Letters of William Thompson Lusk*. New York: privately printed, 1911.

Mahon, Samuel. "The Civil War Letters of Samuel Mahon, Seventh Iowa Infantry." Ed. John K. Mahon. *Iowa Journal of History*, 51 (1953), 233–66.

Martin, John Alexander. "Some Notes on the Eighth Kansas Infantry and the Battle of Chickamauga; Letters of Col. John A. Martin." Ed. Martha B. Caldwell. *Kansas Historical Quarterly*, 13 (1944), 139–45.

McAllister, Robert. *The Civil War Letters of General Robert McAllister*. Ed. James I. Robertson, Jr. New Brunswick, N. J.: Rutgers University Press, 1965.

McClure, Joseph Lewis. "Civil War Letters of William T. and Joseph L. McClure of the Fifteenth Kentucky Volunteer Infantry." Ed. G. Glen Clift. *Register of the Kentucky Historical Society,* 60 (1962), 209–32.

McClure, William T. "Civil War Letters of William T. and Joseph L. McClure of the Fifteenth Kentucky Volunteer Infantry." Ed. G. Glenn Clift. *Register of the Kentucky Historical Society,* 60 (1962), 209–32.

McCrea, Tully. *Dear Belle; Letters from a Cadet and Officer to his Sweetheart, 1858–1865.* Ed. Catherine S. Crary. Middletown, Conn.: Wesleyan University Press, 1965, pp. 124–238.

McMillen, George Washington. "Civil War Letters of George Washington McMillen and Jefferson O. McMillen, 122nd Regiment, O.V.I." *West Virginia History,* 32 (1971), 171–93.

Meade, George Gordon. *The Life and Letters of George Gordon Meade, Major-General United States Army.* Vol. 1. Ed. George Gordon Meade. New York: Scribner's Sons, 1913.

Meagher, Thomas Francis. "Some Letters of General T. F. Meagher." *Journal of the American Irish Historical Society,* 30 (1932), 83–87.

Merrill, Samuel. "Letters from a Civil War Officer." Ed. A. T. Volwiler. *Mississippi Valley Historical Review,* 14 (1928), 508–29.

O'Connor, Henry. "With the First Iowa Infantry." *Palimpsest,* 3 (1922), 53–61.

Orme, William Ward. "Civil War Letters of Brigadier General William Ward Orme, 1862–1866." *Journal of the Illinois Historical Society,* 23 (1930), 246–315.

Partridge, Samuel S. "Civil War Letters of Samuel S. Partridge of the 'Rochester Regiment.'" *Rochester Historical Society Publications* 22 (1944), 77–90.

Perry, John Gardner. *Letters from a Surgeon of the Civil War.* Comp. Martha Derby Perry. Boston: Little, Brown, 1906.

Pierce, Francis Edwin. "Civil War Letters of Francis Edwin Pierce of the 108th New York Volunteer Infantry." *Rochester Historical Society Publications,* 22 (1944), 150–73.

Smith, Thomas Kilby. *Life and Letters of Thomas Kilby Smith, Brevet Major-General United States Volunteers, 1820–1887.* Walter George Smith. New York: G. P. Putnam's Sons, 1898, pp. 169–408.

Stem, Leander. "Stand by the Colors: The Civil War Letters of Leander Stem." Ed. John T. Hubbell. *Register of the Kentucky Historical Society,* 73 (1975), 171–94, 291–313, 396–415.

Stewart, William S. "William S. Stewart Letters, January 13, 1861, to December 4, 1862." Eds. Harvey L. Carter and Norma L. Peterson. *Missouri Historical Review,* 61 (1967), 187–228, 303–20, 463–88.

Taylor, Charles Frederick. "Colonel of the Bucktails: Civil War Letters of Charles Frederick Taylor." Charles F. Hobson and Arnold Shankman. *Pennsylvania Magazine of History and Biography,* 97 (1973), 333–61.

Thrall, Seneca B. "An Iowa Doctor in Blue: Letters of Seneca B. Thrall, 1862–1864." Ed. Mildred Throne. *Iowa Journal of History,* 58 (1960), 97–188.

Weld, Stephen Minot. *War Diary and Letters of Stephen Minot Weld, 1861–1865.* Cambridge, Mass.: Riverside Press, 1912.

Welsh, George Wilson. "Civil War Letters from Two Brothers." *Yale Review,* 18 (1928), 148–61.

Welshimer, Philip. "Letters from Colonel Grant's Regiment." *Ulysses S. Grant Association Newsletter,* 4 (1966), 1–8.

Wilder, John Augustus. "Key West in the Summer of 1864." Ed. Millicent Todd Bingham. *Florida Historical Quarterly,* 43 (1964–65), 262–65.

Williamson, Peter J. "With the First Wisconsin Cavalry, 1862–1865; The Letters of Peter J. Williamson." Ed. Henry Lee Swint. *Wisconsin Magazine of History*, 26 (1943), 333–45, 433–48.

Southern Officers

Archer, James Jay. "The James J. Archer Letters: A Marylander in the Civil War." Ed. C. A. Porter Hopkins. *Maryland Historical Magazine*, 56 (1961), 72–93, 125–49.

Barnes, Ruffin. "The Confederate Letters of Ruffin Barnes of Wilson County." Ed. Hugh Buckner Johnston, Jr. *North Carolina Historical Review*, 31 (1954), 75–99.

Batchelor, Benjamin Franklin. *Batchelor-Turner Letters, 1861–1864, Written by Two of Terry's Texas Rangers*. Annot. H. J. H. Rugeley. Austin, Texas: Steck Co., 1961.

Cage, William L. "The Civil War Letters of William L. Cage." Ed. T. Harry Williams. *Louisiana Historical Quarterly*, 39 (1956), 113–30.

Cameron, Alexander, "A Soldiers Fare is Rough: Letters from A. Cameron in the Indiana Territory, Arkansas Campaign, 1862–1864." Ed. J. S. Duncan. *Military History of Texas and the Southwest*, 12 (1974), 39–61.

Conn, Charles Augustus. "Letters of Two Confederate Officers: William Thomas Conn and Charles Augustus Conn." Ed. T. Conn Bryan. *Georgia Historical Quarterly*, 46 (1962), 169–95.

Conn, William Thomas. "Letters of Two Confederate Officers: William Thomas Conn and Charles Augustus Conn." Ed. T. Conn Bryan. *Georgia Historical Quarterly*, 46 (1962), 169–95.

Crawford, William Ayers. "A Saline Guard: The Civil War Letters of Col. William Ayers Crawford, C.S.A., 1861–1865." Ed. Charles G. Williams. *Arkansas Historical Quarterly*, 31 (1972), 328–55.

Davidson, Charles. "Major Charles A. Davidson: Letters of a Virginia Soldier." Ed. Charles W. Turner. *Civil War History*, 22 (1976), 16–40.

Davidson, John Mitchell. "A Wartime Story: The Davidson Letters, 1862–1865." Ed. Jane Bonner Peacock. *Atlanta History Bulletin*, 19 (1975), 8–121.

Davis, Newton N. "Newton N. Davis Confederate Letters." Contrib. Henry S. Halbert. *Alabama Historical Quarterly*, 18 (1956), 605–10.

Douglas, James P. "The Letters of James P. Douglas to Sallie Susan White, 1861–1865," in *Douglas's Texas Battery, CSA*. Ed. Lucia Rutherford Douglas. Tyler, Texas: Smith County Historical Society, 1966, pp. 1–157.

Duncan, John W. "Letters of John W. Duncan, Captain, Confederate States of America." Ed. Hubert L. Ferguson. *Arkansas Historical Quarterly*, 9 (1950), 298–312.

Dwinnel, Melvin. "Letters of Melvin Dwinnell: Yankee Rebel." Ed. Virginia Griffin Bailey. *Georgia Historical Quarterly*, 47 (1963), 193–203.

Ewell, Richard Stoddert. *The Making of a Soldier; Letters of General R. S. Ewell*. Ed. Percy Gatling Hamlin. Richmond, Va.: Whittet and Shepperson, 1935.

Garner, William Wakefield. "Letters of an Arkansas Confederate Soldier." Ed. D. D. McBrien. *Arkansas Historical Quarterly*, 2 (1943), 58–70, 171–84, 268–86.

Gilliam, Robert C. "From Paraclifta to Marks' Mill: The Civil War Correspondence of Lieutenant Robert C. Gilliam." *Arkansas Historical Quarterly*, 17 (1958), 272–302.

Ginder, Henry. "A Louisiana Engineer at the Seige of Vicksburg: Letters of Henry Ginder." Ed. L. Moody Simms, Jr. *Louisiana History*, 8 (1967), 371–78.

Goodson, Joab. "The Letters of Captain Joab Goodson, 1862–64." Ed. W. Stanley Hoole. *Alabama Review*, 10 (1957), 126–53, 215–31.

Hosford, John W. "A Florida Soldier in the Army of Northern Virginia: The Hosford Letters." Ed. Knox Mellon, Jr. *Florida Historical Quarterly*, 46 (1967–68), 243–71.

Kidd, Reuben. *Reuben Vaughan Kidd, Soldier of the Confederacy*. Alice V. D. Pierrepont. Petersburg, Va.: Violet Bank, 1947, pp. 287–331.

Lang, David. "Civil War Letters of Colonel David Lang." Ed. Bertram H. Groene. *Florida Historical Quarterly*, 54 (1976), 340–66.

Lee, Robert E. *The Wartime Papers of R. E. Lee*. Ed. Clifford Dowdey. New York: Bramhall House, 1961.

Lightfoot, James Newell. "Letters of Three Lightfoot Brothers, 1861–1864." Contrib. Edmund Cody Burnett. *Georgia Historical Quarterly*, 25 (1941), 371–400; 26 (1942), 65–90.

Lynch, James D. "James D. Lynch in War and Peace." James A. Carpenter. *Alabama Historical Quarterly*, 20 (1958), 71–84.

Magee, Warren G. "The Confederate Letters of Warren G. Magee." Ed. Bell Irvin Wiley. *Journal of Mississippi History*, 5 (1943), 204–13.

Mathers, Augustus Henry. "The Civil War Letters of Augustus Henry Mathers, Assistant Surgeon, Fourth Florida Regiment, C.S.A." Ed. Franklin A. Doty. *Florida Historical Quarterly*, 36 (1957–58), 94–124.

Maxwell, David Elwell. "Some Letters to his Parents, by a Floridian in the Confederate Army." Transcrib. Gilbert Wright. *Florida Historical Quarterly*, 36 (1957–58), 353–72.

McGehee, Valentine Merriwether. "Captain Valentine Merriwether M'Gehee." *Publications of the Arkansas Historical Association*, 4 (1917), 140–51.

Miller, Nicholas W. *War Was the Place; A Centenniel Collection of Confederate Soldier Letters*. Old Oakbowery, Chambers Co., Ala.: Chattahoochee Valley Historical Society, Bulletin no. 5, 1961.

Miller, Robert H. "Letters of Lieutenant Robert H. Miller to his Family, 1861–62." Ed. Forrest P. Connor. *Virginia Magazine of History and Biography*, 70 (1962), 62–91.

Mills, Luther Rice. "Letters of Luther Rice Mills, a Confederate Soldier." *North Carolina Historical Review*, 4 (1927), 285–310.

Montfort, Theodorick W. "Rebel Lawyer: The Letters of Lt. Theodorick W. Montfort, 1861–1862." Ed. Spencer Bidwell King, Jr. *Georgia Historical Quarterly*, 48 (1964), 313–33, 451–71; 49 (1965), 82–97, 200–16, 324–34.

Peery, James S. "The Romance of a Man in Gray, Including the Love Letters of Captain James S. Peery, Forty-fifth Virginia Infantry Regiment, C.S.A." Robert Leroy Hilldrup. *West Virginia History*, 22 (1960–61), 83–116, 166–83, 217–39.

Pender, William Dorsey. *The General to His Lady: The Civil War Letters of William W. Dorsey Pender to Fanny Pender*. Ed. William W. Hassler. Chapel Hill: University of North Carolina Press, 1965.

Pendleton, Alexander Swift. "The Valley Campaign of 1862 as Revealed in Letters of Sandie Pendleton." Ed. W. G. Bean. *Virginia Magazine of History and Biography*, 78 (1970), 326–64.

Pickett, George Edward. *Soldier of the South; General Pickett's War Letters to his Wife*. Ed. Arthur Crew Inman. Boston: Houghton Mifflin, 1928.

Polk, L. L. "Colonel L. L. Polk's Wartime Letters to His Wife," in Clarence Poe, *True Tales of the South at War*. Chapel Hill: University of North Carolina Press, 1961, pp. 77–87.

Robison, Hugh Harris. "Hugh Harris Robison Letters," Ed. Weymouth T. Jordan. *Journal of Mississippi History*, 1 (1939), 53–59.
Rogers, William P. "The Diary and Letters of William P. Rogers, 1846–1862." Ed. Eleanor Damon Pace. *Southwestern Historical Quarterly*, 32 (1929), 259–99.
Rowland, Thomas. "Letters of Major Thomas Rowland, C.S.A., From the Camps at Ashland and Richmond, Virginia, 1861." *William and Mary College Quarterly*, 24 (1915–16), 145–153, 232–238; "Letters of Major Thomas Rowland, C.S.A., From North Carolina, 1861 and 1862." *William and Mary College Quarterly*, 25 (1916–17), 73–82, 225–35.

Smith, N. H. "N. H. Smith's Letters from Sabine Pass, 1863." Ed. Alwyn Barr. *East Texas Historical Journal*, 4 (1966), 140–43.
Stannard, Beverly. *Letters of a New Market Cadet*. Eds. John G. Barrett and Robert K. Turner, Jr. Chapel Hill: University of North Carolina Press, 1961.
Steele, Nimrod Hunter. "The Nimrod Hunter Steele Diary and Letters." in *Diaries, Letters, and Recollections of the War Between the States*. Winchester, Va.: Winchester-Frederick County Historical Society Papers, vol. 3, 1955.
Stephens, William Anderson. *War Was the Place; A Centenniel Collection of Confederate Soldier Letters*. Old Oakbowery, Chambers Co., Ala.: Chattahoochee Valley Historical Society, Bulletin no. 5, 1961.
Strayhorn, Thomas Jackson. "Letters of Thomas Jackson Strayhorn." Ed. Henry McGilbert Wagstaff. *North Carolina Historical Review*, 13 (1936), 311–34.
Stuart, James Ewell Brown. *Letters of General J. E. B. Stuart to his Wife, 1861*. Ed. Binham Duncan. Atlanta: The Library, Emory University, 1943.

Walter, William J. "A Louisiana Volunteer; Letters of William J. Walter, 1861–62." Ed. Edwin A. Davis. *Southwest Review*, 19 (1933), 78–87.
Welch, Spencer Glasgow. *A Confederate Surgeon's Letters to his Wife*. 1911; rpt. Marietta, Ga.: Continental Book Co., 1954.
Welsh, John P. "A House Divided: The Civil War Letters of a Virginia Family." W. G. Bean. *Virginia Magazine of History and Biography*, 59 (1951), 397–422.
Wynne, Val. "Civil War Letters to Wynnewood." Walter T. Durham. *Tennessee Historical Quarterly*, 34 (1975), 32–47.

Enlisted Northerners

Adams, John. "Letters of John Adams to Catherine Varner, 1864–1865." *North Dakota Historical Quarterly*, 4 (1929–30), 266–70.
Allen, Amory K. "Civil War Letters of Amory K. Allen." *Indiana Magazine of History*, 31 (1935), 338–86.
Allen, Winthrop S. G. *Civil War Letters of Winthrop S. G. Allen*. Ed. Harry E. Pratt. Springfield, Ill.: Phillips Bros. Printery, 1932.

Ball, Lafayette. "Letters of Privates Cook and Ball." *Indiana Magazine of History*, 27 (1931), 243–68.
Barnett, John Lympus. "Some Civil War Letters and Diary of John Lympus Barnett." Ed. James Barnett. *Indiana Magazine of History*, 37 (1941), 162–73.
Bert, Henry Lawson. "Letters of a Drummer-Boy." Ed. Don Russell. *Indiana Magazine of History*, 34 (1938), 324–39.
Boots, Edward Nichols. "Civil War Letters of E. N. Boots from New Bern and Plymouth." Ed. Wilfred W. Black. *North Carolina Historical Review*, 36 (1959), 205–23. "Civil War Letters of E. N. Boots: Virginia, 1862." Ed. Wilfred W. Black. *Virginia Magazine of History and Biography*, 69 (1961), 194–209.

Bragg, Edwin C. "The Letters of Edwin C. Bragg," in "The Gay Letters: A Civil War Correspondence." Ed. Max L. Heyman. *Journal of the West*, 9 (1970), 377–412.

Brainard, Orson. "Orson Brainard: A Soldier in the Ranks." Ed. Wilfred W. Black. *Ohio History*, 76 (1967), 54–72.

Brown, Benjamin Balmer. "Civil War Letters." *North Dakota Historical Quarterly*, 1, no. 3 (1926–27), 60–71; 1, no. 4, (1926–27), 61–68.

Butterfield, Ira. "The Correspondence of Ira Butterfield." *North Dakota Historical Quarterly*, 3 (1928–29), 129–44.

Carr, Levi. "Documents" [Civil War Letters of Levi Carr]. *North Dakota Historical Quarterly*, 1 (1926–27), 62–64.

Chadwick, Wallace W. "Into the Breach; Civil War Letters of Wallace W. Chadwick." Ed. Mabel Watkins Mayer. *Ohio Historical Quarterly*, 52 (1943), 158–80.

Chase, Charles. "Letters of a Maine Soldier Boy." Norman C. Delaney. *Civil War History*, 5 (1959), 45–61.

Cody, Darwin. "Civil War Letters of Darwin Cody." Ed. Stanley P. Wasson. *Ohio Historical Quarterly*, 68 (1959), 371–407.

Collins, Cordello. "A Bucktail Voice; Civil War Correspondence of Pvt. Cordello Collins." Ed. Mark Reinsberg. *Western Pennsylvania Historical Magazine*, 48 (1965), 235–248.

Cook, Charles N. "Letters of Privates Cook and Ball." *Indiana Magazine of History*, 27 (1931), 243–68.

Cooke, Chauncey Herbert. "A Badger Boy in Blue: The Letters of Chauncey H. Cooke." *Wisconsin Magazine of History*, 4 (1920), 75–100, 208–217, 321–344; 5 (1921), 63–98. (various titles).

Coon, David. "Civil War Letters of David Coon." *North Dakota Historical Quarterly*, 8 (1941), 191–218.

Crumrine, Bishop. "Corporal Crumrine Goes to War." Ed. Walter S. Sanderlin. *Topic*, Fall, 1961, pp. 48–64.

Dunham, Abner. "Civil War Letters of Abner Dunham, 12th Iowa Infantry." Ed. Mildred Throne. *Iowa Journal of History*, 53 (1955), 303–40.

Faller, John I. *Dear Folks at Home: The Civil War Letters of Leo W. and John I. Faller, with an Account of Andersonville*. Ed. Milton E. Flower. Carlisle, Pa.: Cumberland Co. Historical Society and Hamilton Library Association, 1963.

Faller, Leo W. *Dear Folks at Home: The Civil War Letters of Leo W. and John I. Faller, with an Account of Andersonville*. Ed. Milton E. Flower. Carlisle, Pa.: Cumberland Co. Historical Society and Hamilton Library Association, 1963.

Fowle, George. *Letters to Eliza from a Union Soldier, 1862–1865*. Ed. Margaret Greenleaf. Chicago: Follett Publishing Co., 1970.

Gardner, Washington. "Civil War Letters." *Michigan Historical Magazine*, 1, no. 2 (1917), 3–18.

Gay, Samuel Frederick. "The Gay Letters: A Civil War Correspondence." Ed. Max L. Heyman. *Journal of the West*, 9 (1970), 377–412.

Glazier, James E. "The Roanoke Island Expedition: Observations of a Massachusetts Soldier." Ed. James I. Robertson, Jr. *Civil War History*, 12 (1966), 321–46.

Greenalch, James. "Letters of James Greenalch." Ed. Knox Mellon, Jr. *Michigan History*, 44 (1960), 188–240.

Gulick, William O. "Journal and Letters of Corporal William O. Gulick." *Iowa Journal of History*, 28 (1930), 194–267, 390–455, 543–603.

Hollis, Herber R. "Hollis Correspondence." *Indiana Magazine of History*, 36 (1940), 275–94..

Hollis, Joseph H. "Hollis Correspondence." *Indiana Magazine of History*, 36 (1940), 275–94.

Hudson, David Mitchell. "Civil War Letters of David Mitchell Hudson." Contrib. Roy D. Hudson. *Indiana Magazine of History*, 47 (1951), 191–208.

Jackson, Isaac. *"Some of the boys..." The Civil War Letters of Isaac Jackson, 1862–1865.* Ed. Joseph Orville Jackson. Carbondale, Ill.: Southern Illinois University Press, 1960.

Knowles, Frank W. "Hollis Correspondence." *Indiana Magazine of History*, 36 (1940), 275–94.

Litherland, Ebenezer C. "Letters from the Kane County Cavalry." Ed. Clifford Egan. *Lincoln Herald*, 45 (1963), 144–49.

Malcolm, Frank. "'Such is War': The Letters of an Orderly in the 7th Iowa Infantry." Ed. James I. Robertson, Jr. *Iowa Journal of History*, 58 (1960), 321–56.

Marshall, Henry. "Civil War Letters of Henry Marshall." *North Dakota Historical Quarterly*, 9 (1941), 35–57.

McMillen, Jefferson O. "Civil War Letters of George Washington McMillen and Jefferson O. McMillen, 122nd Regiment, O.V.I." *West Virginia History*, 32 (1971), 171–93.

Meade, Rufus. "With Sherman through Georgia and the Carolinas: Letters of a Federal Soldier." Ed. James A. Padgett. *Georgia Historical Quarterly*, 32 (1948), 285–322; 33 (1949), 49–81.

Newton, James K. *A Wisconsin Boy in Dixie; The Selected Letters of James K. Newton.* Ed. Stephen E. Ambrose. Madison, Wisc.: University of Wisconsin Press, 1961.

Olivett, John M. "A New Yorker in Florida in 1862: War Letters of John M. Olivett to his Sister in Dutchess County." Ed. James P. Jones. *New York History*, 42 (1961), 169–175.

Rawalt, John. "The Civil War Correspondence of John Rawalt of Illinois." Robert E. Levinson. *Lincoln Herald*, 72 (1970), 96–103.

Reid, Harvey. *The View from Headquarters; Civil War Letters of Harvey Reid.* Ed. Frank L. Byrne. Madison: State Historical Society of Wisconsin, 1965.

Remington, Ambert O. "The Occupation of Southeastern Louisiana: Impressions of a New York Volunteer, 1862–1863." L. Moody Simms, Jr. *Louisiana Studies*, 7 (1968), 83–91.

Reynolds, Nathaniel M. "The Civil War Letters of Nathaniel M. Reynolds." Ed. James Barnett. *Lincoln Herald*, 65 (1963), 199–213.

Rollins, George S. "'Give My Love to All': The Civil War Letters of George S. Rollins." Ed. Gerald S. Henig. *Civil War Times Illustrated*, 11, no. 7 (1972), 16–28.

Rumple, John. "Ohiowa Soldier." Ed. H. E. Rosenberger. *Annals of Iowa*, 3rd Ser. 36 (1961), 111–148.

Sharp, John. "The Sharp Family Civil War Letters." Ed. George Mills. *Annals of Iowa*, 3rd Ser. 34 (1959), 481–532.

Shelly, Joseph Frederick. "The Shelly Letters." Ed. Fanny J. Anderson. Trans. Sophie S. Gemant. *Indiana Magazine of History*, 44 (1948), 181–98.

Snure, Samuel E. "The Vicksburg Campaign as Viewed by an Indiana Soldier." Ed. William A. Russ, Jr. *Journal of Mississippi History*, 19 (1957), 263–69.

Stallcop, James. "Letters of James Stallcop to Catherine Varner, Charlotte, Iowa, 1863–65." *North Dakota Historical Quarterly*, 4 (1929–30), 116–42.

Welsh, James. "A House Divided: The Civil War Letters of a Virginia Family." Ed. W. G. Bean. *Virginia Magazine of History and Biography*, 59 (1951), 397–422.

Welsh, Philip R. "Civil War Letters from Two Brothers." *Yale Review*, 18 (1928), 148–61.
Wilson, Peter. "Peter Wilson in the Civil War." *Iowa Journal of History*, 40 (1942), 153–203, 261–320, 339–414.
Wise, George M. "Civil War Letters of George M. Wise." Ed. Wilfred W. Black. *Ohio Historical Quarterly*, 65 (1956), 53–81; "Marching Through South Carolina: Another Civil War Letter of Lieutenant George M. Wise." *Ohio Historical Quarterly*, 66 (1957), 187–95.
Woodford, Milton M. "A Connecticut Yankee Fights at Olustee: Letters From the Front." Ed. Vaughn D. Bornet. *Florida Historical Quarterly*, 27 (1948–49), 237–59; "A Connecticut Yankee After Olustee." *Florida Historical Quarterly*, 27 (1948–49), 385–403.

Enlisted Southerners

Affleck, Dunbar. "With Terry's Texas Rangers: The Letters of Dunbar Affleck." Eds. Robert W. Williams, Jr., and Ralph A. Wooster. *Civil War History*, 9 (1963), 299–319.
Alspangh, Granville L. "Letters of a Confederate Soldier, 1862–1863." Ed. Mary Elizabeth Sanders. *Louisiana Historical Quarterly*, 29 (1946), 1229–40.

Banks, Robert Webb. "The Civil War Letters of Robert W. Banks." Ed. George C. Osborn. *Journal of Mississippi History*, 5 (1943), 141–54.
Batts, William. "A Foot Soldier's Account: Letters of William Batts, 1861–1862." Ed. Jane Bonner Peacock, *Georgia Historical Quarterly*, 50 (1966), 87–100.
Boyd, Casper. "Casper W. Boyd, Company I. 15th Alabama Infantry, C.S.A., A Casualty of the Battle of Cross Keys, Virginia, His Last Letters Written Home." *Alabama Historical Quarterly*, 23 (1961), 291–99.
Bridges, Richard C. "Letters from Private Richard C. Bridges, C.S.A., 1861–1864." Ed. William L. Huettel. *Journal of Mississippi History*, 33 (1971), 357–372.

Cadenhead, I. B. "Some Confederate Letters of I. B. Cadenhead; Co. H., 34th Alabama Infantry Regiment." *Alabama Historical Quarterly*, 18 (1956), 564–71.
Cochrane, Harden Perkins. "The Letters of Harden Perkins Cochrane, 1862–1864." Arr. Harriet Fitts Ryan. *Alabama Review*, 7 (1954), 277–94; 8 (1955), 55–70, 143–52, 219–28, 277–90.
Cody, Barnett Hardeman. "Letters of Barnett Hardeman Cody and Others, 1861–1864." Contrib. Edmund Cody Burnett. *Georgia Historical Quarterly*, 23 (1939), 265–99, 362–80.
Cotton, John Weaver. "The Civil War Letters of John W. Cotton." Ed. Lucille Griffith. *Alabama Review*, 3 (1950), 207–31. 286–99.
Cotton, Joseph A. "The Cotton Letters." *Virginia Historical Magazine*, 37 (1929), 12–22.

Dorman, Jesse C. *War Was the Place; A Centenniel Collection of Confederate Soldier Letters.* Old Oakbowery, Chambers Co., Ala.: Chattahoochee Valley Historical Society, Bulletin no. 5, 1961.
Dunn, Matthew Andrew. "Matthew Andrew Dunn Letters." Ed. Weymouth T. Jordan. *Journal of Mississippi History*, 1 (1939), 110–27.

Fall, Albert Boult. "Civil War Letters of Albert Boult Fall; Gunner for the Confederacy." *Register of the Kentucky Historical Society*, 59 (1961), 150–68.
Fay, Edwin H. *"This Infernal War"; The Confederate Letters of Sgt. Edwin H. Fay.* Ed. Bell Irvin Wiley. Austin, Texas: University of Texas Press, 1958.

Handerson, Henry Ebenezer. *Yankee in Gray; The Civil War Memoirs of Henry E. Handerson, with a Selection of his Wartime Letters.* Intro. Clyde L. Cummer. Cleveland: Press of Western Reserve University, 1962.

Hightower, Harvey Judson. "Letters from H. J. Hightower, a Confederate Soldier, 1862–1864." Ed. Dewey W. Grantham, Jr. *Georgia Historical Quarterly,* 40 (1956), 174–89.

Hodnett, John W. *War Was the Place; A Centenniel Collection of Confederate Soldier Letters.* Old Oakbowery, Chambers Co., Ala.: Chattahoochee Valley Historical Society, Bulletin no. 5, 1961.

Holt, Hiram T. "'The Momentous Events' of the Civil War as Reported by a Confederate Private-Sergeant." Robert Partin. *Tennessee Historical Quarterly,* 18 (1959), 69–86.

Huckaby, Leander. "A Mississippian in Lee's Army: The Letters of Leander Huckaby." Ed. Donald E. Reynolds. *Journal of Mississippi History,* 36 (1974), 53–67, 165–78, 272–88.

Kibler, James Allen. "Letters from a Confederate Soldier." *Tyler's Quarterly,* 31 (1949–50), 120–27.

Lee, E. Jefferson. "A Collection of Louisiana Confederate Letters." Ed. Frank E. Vandiver. *Louisiana Historical Quarterly,* 26 (1943), 937–74.

Lee, George M. "A Collection of Louisiana Confederate Letters." Ed. Frank E. Vandiver. *Louisiana Historical Quarterly,* 26 (1943), 937–74.

Lightfoot, Thomas Reese. "Letters of Three Lightfoot Brothers, 1861–1864." Contrib. Edmund Cody Burnett. *Georgia Historical Quarterly,* 25 (1941), 371–400; 26 (1942), 65–90.

Lightfoot, William Edwin. "Letters of Three Lightfoot Brothers, 1861–1864." Contrib. Edmund Cody Burnett. *Georgia Historical Quarterly,* 25 (1941), 371–400; 26 (1942), 65–90.

Lovelace, Lucius Todd Cicero. *War Was the Place; A Centenniel Collection of Confederate Soldier Letters.* Old Oakbowery, Chambers Co., Ala.: Chattahoochee Valley Historical Society, Bulletin no. 5, 1961.

McDermid, Angus. "Letters from a Confederate Soldier." Benjamin Rountree. *Georgia Review,* 18 (1964), 267–97.

McRaven, David Olando. "The Correspondence of David Olando McRaven and Amanda Nantz McRaven, 1864–1865." Ed. Louis A. Brown. *North Carolina Historical Review,* 26 (1949), 41–98.

Merz, Louis. *War Was the Place; A Centenniel Collection of Confederate Soldier Letters.* Old Oakbowery, Chambers Co., Ala.: Chattahoochee Valley Historical Society, Bulletin no. 5, 1961.

Miller, John W. *War Was the Place; A Centenniel Collection of Confederate Soldier Letters.* Old Oakbowery, Chambers Co., Ala.: Chattahoochee Valley Historical Society, Bulletin no. 5, 1961.

Murphree, Joel Dyer. "Autobiography and Civil War Letters of Joel Murphree of Troy, Alabama, 1864–1865." Intro. H. E. Sterkx. *Alabama Historical Quarterly,* 19 (1957), 170–208.

Newberry, Thomas Jefferson. "The Civil War Letters of Thomas Jefferson Newberry." Ed. Enoch L. Mitchell. *Journal of Mississippi History,* 10 (1948), 44–80.

O'Daniel, W. J. "The Road to Gettysburg; The Diary and Letters of Leonidas Torrence of the Gaston Guards." Ed. Haskell Monroe. *North Carolina Historical Review,* 36 (1959), 476–517.;

Orr, Henry. *Campaigning with Parsons' Texas Cavalry Brigade, CSA; The War Journals and Letters of the Four Orr Brothers, 12th Texas Cavalry Regiment.* Ed. John Q. Anderson. Waco, Texas: Hill Junior College Press, n.d.

Orr, James. *Campaigning with Parsons' Texas Cavalry Brigade, CSA; The War Journals and Letters of the Four Orr Brothers, 12th Texas Cavalry Regiment.* Ed. John Q. Anderson. Waco, Texas: Hill Junior College Press, n.d.
Orr, Lafayette. *Campaigning with Parsons' Texas Cavalry Brigade, CSA; The War Journals and Letters of the Four Orr Brothers, 12th Texas Cavalry Regiment.* Ed. John Q. Anderson. Waco, Texas: Hill Junior College Press, n.d.

Pugh, Richard Lloyd. "A Confederate Artilleryman at Shiloh." Barnes F. Lathrop. *Civil War History,* 8 (1962), 373–85.

Rumph, Langdon Leslie. "Letters of a Teenage Confederate." Ed. Henry Eugene Sterkx and Brooks Thompson. *Florida Historical Quarterly,* 38 (1959–60), 339–46.

Smith, Robert Alexander. "Robert Alexander Smith; A Southern Son." William Robert Stevenson. *Alabama Historical Quarterly,* 20 (1958), 35–60.
Starr, Frank. "New Mexico Campaign Letters of Frank Starr, 1861–1862." Ed. David B. Gracy, II. *Texas Military History,* 4 (1964), 169–88.
Stoker, William Elisha. "The War Letters of a Texas Conscript in Arkansas." Ed. Robert W. Glover. *Arkansas Historical Quarterly,* 20 (1961), 355–87.
Stone, Benjamin. "'My Love to Them All': The Letters of Private Benjamin Stone, C.S.A., to His Sister." Clifford C. Norse. *Mississippi Quarterly,* 23 (1970), 175–79.
Suddath, James Butler. "From Sumter to the Wilderness: Letters of Sergeant James Butler Suddath, Co. E, 7th Regiment S.C.V." Ed. Frank B. Williams, Jr. *South Carolina Historical Magazine,* 63 (1962), 1–11, 93–104.

Thompson, James Thomas. "A Georgia Boy with 'Stonewall' Jackson; The Letters of James Thomas Thompson." Ed. Aurelia Austin. *Virginia Magazine of History and Biography,* 70 (1962), 314–31.
Torrence, Leonidas. "The Road to Gettysburg; The Diary and Letters of Leonidas Torrence of the Gaston Guards." Ed. Haskell Monroe. *North Carolina Historical Review,* 36 (1959), 476–517.
Truss, John. "Civil War Letters from Parsons' Texas Cavalry Brigade." Ed. Johnette Highsmith Ray. *Southwestern Historical Quarterly,* 69 (1965–66), 210–23.
Turner, George Quincy. *Batchelor-Turner Letters, 1861–1864, Written by Two of Terry's Texas Rangers.* Annot. H. J. H. Rugeley. Austin, Texas: Steck Co., 1961.

West John C. *A Texan in Search of a Fight. Being the Diary and Letters of a Private Soldier in Hood's Texas Brigade.* Intro. Col. Harold B. Simpson. 1901; rpt. Waco, Texas: Texian Press, 1969.
Wilson, Joseph David. "A Young Confederate Stationed in Texas; The Letters of Joseph David Wilson, 1864–65." Elvis E. Fleming. *Texana,* 8 (1970), 352–61.
Wilson, Robert T. "Some Hard Fighting; Letters of Private Robert T. Wilson, 5th Texas Infantry, Hood's Brigade, 1862–1864." Elvis. E. Fleming. *Military History of Texas and the Southwest,* 9 (1971), 289–302.

Index